The Penn State Series in German Literature

The Penn State Series in German Literature

General Editor
   Joseph P. Strelka, The Pennsylvania State University

Editorial Board
   Stuart Atkins, University of California at Santa Barbara
   Peter Demetz, Yale University
   Reinhold Grimm, University of Wisconsin
   Erich Heller, Northwestern University
   Victor Lange, Princeton University
   Henry Remak, Indiana University
   Walter Sokel, Stanford University
   Blake Lee Spahr, University of California at Berkeley

German Baroque Poetry 1618–1723, by Robert M. Browning

*War, Weimar, and Literature: The Story of the Neue Merkur,
1914–1926*, by Guy Stern

Kafka's Narrative Theater

Kafka's Narrative Theater

James Rolleston

The Pennsylvania State University Press

University Park and London

Library of Congress Cataloging in Publication Data

Rolleston, James, 1939–
  Kafka's narrative theater.

  (The Penn State series in German literature)
  Bibliography: p.
  1. Kafka, Franz, 1883–1924. I. Title.
II. Series.
PT2621.A26Z864   833'.9'12   73–12574
ISBN 0–271–01121–1

Designed by Glenn Ruby

For three ladies
My mother, my wife, and my daughter

Contents

Acknowledgments

This book was conceived and largely written in 1970 and 1971, when I was the recipient of a Morse Fellowship from Yale University. After preparatory work in London, I was able to write under ideal circumstances in the small town of Sharon, Massachusetts, which boasts, in its town square, the office of a law firm: Kafka, Kaufman, Kafka and Kafka. That the conditions under which I worked were so unlike those encountered by Franz Kafka's characters is chiefly due to my wife, Priscilla, and her indispensable relatives, Anne and Edwin Hall.

I want to thank above all Joseph Strelka, editor of the Penn State Series in German Literature, and my teacher and colleague, Peter Demetz, whose advice and careful reading of the manuscript have played a vital role in its attaining existence as a book. I also recall with special pleasure a talk in Prague with his father, Hans Demetz, whose knowledge of Kafka-lore seems inexhaustible; and valuable discussions in the garden of Emmanuel College, Cambridge, with my former tutor Ronald Gray. Over the years, too, conversations with Heinrich and Ingeborg Henel have taught me the need for an approach to Kafka's works that will do justice to the subtle blend of intellectual and emotional elements in his exploration of the human mind.

J.L.R.
New Haven, 1973

Introduction

In the history of Kafka criticism one of the most significant events was the enunciation by Friedrich Beissner[1] in 1952 of the principle of restricted perspective. Kafka the author, while not identical with his hero, knows no more than the hero does, and compels the reader to share the hero's obsessions by excluding all other perspectives on events. The effect of this insight was to focus critical attention on Kafka the literary craftsman rather than Kafka the anthologist of despair. Such, however, is the theological tendency in Kafka studies that Beissner's remarks became themselves elevated into a dogma, producing in the 1960s the inevitable crop of heretics.[2] Indeed, perhaps because Kafka is so radical a writer, calling into question all categories, ethical and psychological as well as literary, it seems difficult if not impossible to approach him critically without a certain predisposition as to his "meaning"; as Jörgen Kobs notes in a recent overview[3] of books on Kafka, many studies declare themselves exclusively concerned with Kafka "the artist"—only to revert to the unending quest for a metaphysical pattern in his works.

While I cannot claim exemption from this rule, the purpose of the present study is to confront the primary question of how to read Kafka, how to enter his world without a preconceived idea about what will be found there. I have adopted a chronological approach to his work that consciously eschews the impulse to explain the early in terms of the late, the work in terms of the life, allowing instead the problems of Kafka as a writer of fictions to emerge in the context of the state of the art as he found it and his own growing list of contributions to it. As a corollary to this approach I have resisted the temptation, held out by the obsessive interconnectedness of Kafka's writings, to formulate a "key" that would unlock the meaning of everything he said; rather, I have tried to analyze certain of his important fictional undertakings as worlds in their own right, unpredictable even in retrospect. Only thus can one legitimately attempt to define the author's "intention," which Hirsch[4] has shown to be the only secure goal of criticism.

The one point where the focus temporarily shifts occurs in the chapter devoted primarily to Kafka's reactions to the Yiddish theater, as expressed in his diary for 1911–12. The unusual emphasis on this episode is given support by a recent book, *Kafka and the Yiddish Theatre*, by Evelyn Torton Beck,[5] which may become as significant a milestone in Kafka criticism as Beissner's 1952 lecture. So much work on Kafka is speculative; Mrs. Beck has demonstrated tangible links between the Yiddish plays Kafka saw and scenes in stories he wrote later. As is perhaps to be expected from the uncoverer of so important an influence, Beck tends to claim too much, "explaining" Kafka's stories in terms of the actual ethos of the Yiddish plays. Nevertheless her discoveries add a dimension to our understanding of Kafka's creative process; and my discussion of the "theatrical" element in his narrative technique can be seen as a commentary, from a more intrinsic perspective, on the questions raised by her book.[6]

In a rare reference to his own literary techniques on 9 February 1915, Kafka spoke of the need to synthesize "the two elements—most pronounced in 'The Stoker' and 'In the Penal Colony' . . . (die beiden Elemente—am ausgeprägtesten im *Heizer* und in der *Strafkolonie* . . .)."[7] Many critics have theorized about the nature of the two "elements"; an impressive recent formulation is by Malcolm Pasley, who differentiates between "the controlled flow of evocative pictures" and "a technique of deliberate allusion."[8] I share Pasley's view that Kafka was probably referring to the formal problems of verbal creation; my own consideration of the elements as contrasting structural potentialities has taken me beyond a static definition to a renewed discussion of what, if anything, we understand by "development" in Kafka's writing. Periodizations such as Sokel's,[9] that derive essentially from the overt content, seem to violate the tone of detached craftsmanship that imbues even such obsessive stories as "The Judgment" and "In the Penal Colony"; moreover, the essential dividing line between biographical material and the fictional enterprise tends to become blurred. Formalistic approaches, on the other hand, like the attempt by Heinz Hillmann[10] to assimilate Kafka's works into categories based on the traditional genres, neglect the all-pervading presence of the "Kafka hero," the fictional voice identified by Heinz Politzer[11] as the "bachelor" of the earlier diary entries.

The close readings that follow are based on two interlocking premises. The first is that the very creation of a protagonist is a radical act in the light of Kafka's deep-rooted skepticism concerning both external phenomena and human identity; Kafka's unchanging theme is the improbability of existence itself, and the voices of his central characters constitute a fusion of this basic improbability with the irrationally persistent tendencies of the human world towards self-assertion and self-justification. In this respect no development is possible: K. in *The Castle* is no closer to the articulation of a stable identity than the narrator of "Description of a Struggle." But my second premise is that, as Kafka's own remark about the two elements implies, each achieved story becomes a component of the context in which subsequent protagonists are conceived. To borrow the image Kafka himself derived from the Chinese Wall, although there is no logical, sequential relationship between one fictional block and the next, the growing context of existing blocks suggests reasons, however opaque, for the remoteness as well as the proximity of later sitings. It should be possible to isolate the structural patterns struggling to emerge as well as those already established by the irresistibility of Kafka's individual achievements.

A word about terminology. For Kafka the theatrical metaphor is implicit in the very act of writing. Only by postulating a speaker can he make a statement about the world; but the fact of a speaker turns all statements into questions about the speaker's own existence. The speaker and his world come simultaneously into existence on an experimental basis. But although the initiation of the relationship between self and world is arbitrary, the process of that relationship is not. Once the lights go up on this theater of the self, a fundamental law governs the performance: denial of the speaker's expectations. This law, and the maintenance of the speaker's perspective, represent the constants in Kafka's fiction. The variables arise from the hero's view of the world which he defines and which defines him. His attitude, itself a function of the initial situation, generates the story's shape.

To describe the two basic formal tendencies I use the terms "open" and "closed" structure. These terms are derived from Wölfflin; a sentence of his on "open form" has a resonance applicable to my usage:

> The baroque, however, consciously emphasises one side, and thus, since the really unbalanced is no longer art, creates the relation of oscillating balance.[12]

The hero of the open structure is on "one side," on the outside looking in: his position impels him towards the restoration of balance and coherence. Without insisting on a central role, he nevertheless predicates his identity on the affirmation of a logically functioning world; in a word, he seeks continuity. The hero of the closed structure, on the other hand, is cast unwillingly in the central role of a drama beyond his control. He seeks disengagement, narcissistic neutrality, a world in which his own trivializing masks remain in place. But the aesthetics of paradox that govern Kafka's narrative theater ensure that the hero is systematically deprived of the role he craves. The hero of the open structure does indeed generate a "story," but it is the story of his own existence, eluding all congruence with his presumptions about an ordered world; while the hero of the closed structure is forced into the public realm, unable to evade meaning and accusation in the most indifferent gestures and the most "private" spheres of life.

I have adopted one particular procedure that is open to question. The central position in Kafka's oeuvre occupied by his three novels makes the omission of any one of them hard to justify in an overall study, even one that confines itself to selected texts. At the same time the need to stay continuously inside Kafka's worlds as they come into being is so important to my approach that the novels could not be discussed in their entirety without expansion of the study to indigestible lengths. Therefore, taking my cue from Kafka's separate publication of "The Stoker," I have analyzed only the first chapter of each novel, referring freely to later parts of the work, but seeking to elucidate the rhythms through which the protagonist is given fictional life within the confines of the opening chapter.[13] In the case of *The Trial* the procedure is easily justified: the self-contained quality of the chapters, especially the first and last ones, has often been noticed. *The Castle* poses a different problem: Pasley has demonstrated that the chapter divisions as we have them were set arbitrarily, and sometimes illogically, by Max Brod.[14] However, the novel's open-endedness, its apparent independence of chapter-rhythm, is itself remarkable in the light of Kafka's previous practice. My interpretation accepts Brod's division as a starting point, but avoids the kind of "structural" analysis against which Pasley rightly warns in the context of *The Castle*. Indeed, the differences between the two novels and the paradoxical openness of *The Castle* are matters of prime importance for the conclusions of my study.

1 "Description of a Struggle"

The governing image of Kafka's first extant work, "Description of a Struggle (Beschreibung eines Kampfes),"[1] occurs near the end, in a passage later published separately (with unimportant changes)[2] as one of his *Meditations* (*Betrachtungen*):

> For we are like tree trunks in the snow. They lie there apparently flat on the ground and it looks as though one could push them away with a slight kick. But no, one can't, for they are firmly stuck to the ground. But look, even that is only apparent.[3]

Illusion and reality can no longer be distinguished; but Kafka's voices, as the frequency of "organizing" words like "for" and "but" suggests, cannot abandon the incessant, fruitless attempt to make just such distinctions. And yet (to stay within Kafka's mode of presentation) this seemingly arid analytic process can result in a passage such as "tree trunks in the snow" which sums up the impossibility of the situation in such a manner that a form of "reality" is achieved after all, a reality latent in the paradoxical potentialities of language.

Jörgen Kobs, in his recent monumental study, has demonstrated that the linguistic structures achieved by Kafka systematically undercut their own drive towards objectivity: the incessantly observing and analyzing Kafka-hero succeeds only in dislodging ideas and objects from any context outside language itself. But, convincing as Kobs's argument is, it does not "solve" the probably insoluble "Kafka problem." Two points, in particular, demand renewed attention: Kafka's literary origins and the unremitting self-assertion of his heroes. Although Kobs shows that Kafka cannot, even in his early work, be considered in any sense a "naturalist," neither was he functioning in a literary vacuum. Kafka reached maturity at a time when literature was dominated by theory, or rather theories: self-consciously, fiction embodied a wide variety of paths toward the goal of absolute mimesis, from the "objectivity" of Flaubert and Henry James to early stream-of-consciousness (Schnitzler, *Leutnant Gustl*). One can discern a Kafka-like rhythm in the correlation between the self-conscious pursuit of "naturalness" and the ever-increasing complexity of literary artifice. But, as Wayne Booth argues, the problem was essentially in the mind of the writers; far from invalidating his fictional statement, the author's presence is a precondition of its effectiveness:

> It is easy for us now to see what was not so clear at the beginning of the century: whether an impersonal novelist hides behind a single narrator or observer, the multiple points of view of *Ulysses* or *As I Lay Dying*, or the objective surfaces of *The Awkward Age* . . . the author's voice is never really silenced. It is, in fact, one of the things we read fiction for . . . .[4]

In fact the movement away from mimesis was already under way in the fine arts, with the phenomenon of cubism. The impact of cubism derived not only from flouting the viewer's mimetic expectations, but also from the incorporation of "realistic" detail into an antirealistic context. Kafka, too, saw the possibilities of fiction in precisely this antithetical yet congruent relationship with the mimetic modes of his time. Such a view of Kafka might seem unduly "dynamic"; but it does lead to a hypothesis concerning the self-studying, intent personae of Kafka's earlier heroes. The problem of artistic creation has often been mentioned as the underlying "theme" of Kafka's later stories: in the case of his earliest writings it is more than a theme, it is the generative force shaping the narrative techniques that will eventually absorb the eruption of "The Judgment." As the early Kafka hero seeks to establish a "world," he is hoping thereby to guarantee an existence for himself: but since the substance of the world is wholly dependent on his voice, a circle is created which he seeks to break by injecting tension, polarity, into the relationship between himself and the world. Creation and destruction, assertion and denial become the very substance of the notion of identity as it is dismantled, analyzed, and momentarily reconstituted in "Description of a Struggle."

Kafka made it his paradoxical purpose to convey not just feelings but also their underlying negation. He formulated his youthful aim later on in a vividly suggestive passage:

I went over the wishes that I wanted to realize in life. I found that the most important or the most delightful was the wish to attain a view of life (and—this was necessarily bound up with it—to convince others of it in writing), in which life, while still retaining its natural full-bodied rise and fall, would simultaneously be recognized no less clearly as a nothing, a dream, a dim hovering. A beautiful wish, perhaps, if I had wished it rightly. Considered as a wish, somewhat as if one were to hammer together a table with painful and methodical technical efficiency, and simultaneously do nothing at all, and not in such a way that people could say: "Hammering a table together is nothing to him," but rather "Hammering a table together is really hammering a table together to him, but at the same time it is nothing," whereby certainly the hammering would have become still bolder, still surer, still more real and, if you will, still more senseless.[5]

The purpose of "Description of a Struggle" is implicit in these antithetical images: to construct an entertainment while systematically removing all the props which the reader is initially invited to lean on in the usual way—continuity, character, atmosphere, irony, meaning, ideas. These elements are all very much present, even prominent, but they are ceaselessly being canceled and superseded by means of antithesis. This is obvious enough in the second part, the "Diversions (Belustigungen)," for there the interplay between "illusion" and "reality" is brought into the open; but it is also worth examining in the opening pages, which differ much more widely in the two extant versions, and in which Kafka toys with the mimetic styles prevalent in his youth, with impressionism, scientific naturalism, and the reserved precision of Flaubert.

The first two paragraphs, virtually identical in the two versions, immediately make the reader uneasy, like a carefully made photograph that seems to be deliberately out of focus. The consciously fussy detailing surrounding "a few people (einige Leute)," and especially the phrase "said it had been a pleasant evening (sagten, es wäre sehr schön gewesen)," suggest the sardonic manner of Flaubert: the reader settles comfortably into an indictment of petty-bourgeois customs. But this style, which depends on the impersonality of the narrator, is then superseded by the presence of an "I (Ich)." The reader adjusts—the bourgeoisie are not going to be put under the microscope, but dissected from the bitter viewpoint of the melancholy outsider. But the "Ich" seems only interested in savoring the liqueur and pastry on his table;

he is no different from the group in the first paragraph, except that he is alone. Who then has been applying the Flaubertian perspective of the opening lines? Where is the narrator who will clarify matters? Actually there is no confusion; the text could hardly be more lucid. It just refuses to accept the limitations of any one category. All the methods devised by fiction for presenting a given reality have some merit; the author proposes to use them all and leave the reader to grapple with the text that results, an enigma without complexity.

There is no key that will lock all the perspectives into place. One sentence may seem to be canceling the meaning of its predecessor, but in fact it is, quite literally, following it—one sequence of words with a given meaning, placed on the printed page after a sequence with a quite different meaning. The symbolist idea of art as an independent verbal construct lies behind this method, but Kafka is not interested in verbal mysticism. He is not writing a prose poem, although a passage like "tree trunks in the snow" shows him willing and able to incorporate such techniques into the whole. His theme is the relationship between subjectivity and the external world. This relationship having demonstrably broken down, he is unwilling to make any assumptions that would falsify the total fluidity of the situation. Subjectivity is everything and it is nothing, and its fragility is the more apparent, the more whimsically "independent" of the world it chooses to become. As Judith Ryan emphasizes: "The very possibility of being an individual is here at stake—not the development of individuality in conflict with an external world."[6] The "bottomless" quality Beda Allemann has discerned in the opening sentence of *The Trial*[7] originates in the discontinuities of the present work.

Having set the scene in a way calculated to sow doubts about the spiritual location of his first-person narrator, Kafka now launches a hasty and banal personal relationship. The purpose of the two speeches seems to be to negate the initial description by the narrator of the new arrival as an "acquaintance." The acquaintance specifically disclaims being such; both speeches are a collection of formal phrases that seem unconnected with what the speakers are actually thinking about ("smiling absent-mindedly at my occupation . . . I looked at him sadly—the piece of fruitcake which I had in my mouth did not taste particularly good . . . .").[8] Finally, the narrator's words appear to constitute a withdrawal from any relationship. Already, however, Kafka is using conjunctions like "but" and "for" incongruously in order to undermine the idea of causality by drawing attention to meaningless examples of it. This now comes into the open with the absurd sentence beginning, "When I had said this, he sat down . . . (Als ich das gesagt hatte, setzte er sich . . .).'" Although *als* is not a specifically causal word, we are accustomed to finding an orderly connection between subordinate and main clauses. Here there is none; *als* is stripped down to its bare sequential meaning. Or is it? Perhaps, as we are to find explicitly stated in the "Diversions," the acquaintance regards discouraging remarks as the warmest kind of welcome. But one must beware of setting up any kind of reverse causality, remembering the line from "tree trunks in the snow": "even that is only apparent (sogar das ist bloss scheinbar)."

The description of the acquaintance's posture as he speaks seems pointless, and indeed it is; but like the other stylistic blind alleys, it has a function at the given moment in the author's campaign of disruption. Here the purpose of the precisely "observed" detail appears to be to build up an atmosphere in which the reader can be seduced into believing in the "characters" and taking a few comfortable steps down the reductionist path. To knock down a response, Kafka must first set it up; and the notion of character is one of his preoccupations in this story. Can we assemble the narrator's actions and reactions into a coherent "character"? Should we try to do so? Can we avoid trying to do so? Here the acquaintance is built up for several paragraphs into a fairly stock figure, the drunk who insists on divulging his amorous experiences, and this throws into relief all the more the strangeness of the narrator. This strangeness becomes vivid when Kafka undermines the idea of causality in language still further with the word "therefore" in "Therefore I stood up (Daher stand ich auf)".[9] Again, it is not that there is *no* explanation for the narrator's response; Kafka never allows his narrative to veer into the plainly irrational, for that would release the reader from his predicament. But the approach of some yawning gentlemen attracted by the drunk's outpourings would not "naturally" provoke an invitation to the latter to take a long walk in midwinter. There is no suggestion that the narrator finds his acquaintance appealing (various positive and negative reactions occur later). The reader may weakly decide that he is "shy" and utters such speeches when embarrassed; and in the second version Kafka has elaborated the passage a little and added a colloquial tone to lend seeming support to this interpretation. But there remains something cool and unapproachable in the language that reminds us of the logical but impenetrable heroes of Kafka's later novels. The "congruence" which Martin Walser discerns between author's and hero's perspective in the major novels applies here too. Just as we do not "know" Josef K., but rather make deductions about him from the way he reports events (and vice versa; the significance of the events is inseparable from Josef K.'s "character"), so the inconsequential and bizarre events of "Description" are reflected in and by the unpredictable and essentially fragmented character of the narrator.

Following the shock effect of the little word "therefore" Kafka allows the reader five paragraphs of more or less conventional story-telling (in which the narrator is significantly uninvolved except to give the servant girl money) until the uniquely Kafka-like appearance of the adverb "evidently (offenbar)" in "Hardly were we outside when I evidently began to feel very gay."[10] Dorrit Cohn, investigating the switch from first- to third-person narration in the early chapters of the *Castle* manuscript,[11] remarks that Kafka made virtually no alterations in sentence structure, that sentences like the following occur in the original version: "Again I stopped, as if, by standing still, I had more power of judgment."[12] Cohn regards the excessive openness, the unsettling effect on perspective of such sentences as the reason Kafka made the change to the third person; and in the context of *The Castle* she is probably right, as consistency of perspective is an important element in the novel. But that Kafka could pen such sentences in his last years emphasizes that the speculative viewpoint, the sudden and recurrent "alienation" from the self, is a potential or actual component of his work from "Description of a Struggle" onwards.[13] Indeed, the disjunction between the "observer" and the "doer" within the same consciousness is an explicit theme of "Wedding Preparations in the Country (Hochzeitsvorbereitungen auf dem Lande)," another early work; there it is summed up in the striking image of Raban as a large beetle lying in bed while he sends his "fully dressed body (angekleideten Körper)" about his business. Within the context of this dream image Raban can propose a simple causal explanation for his sense of alienation from his own emotions, an explanation that conforms perfectly with Kafka's early intention of postulating a narrative voice grounded in a rhythm of absolute division between feeling and action:

> If it lurches when leaving my room, the lurching provides proof, not of fear, but of its nothingness. It is also no evidence of excitement if it stumbles over the threshold, travels sobbing to the country and, weeping still, eats its dinner there. For as for myself, I am lying in bed all the time.[14]

But even in fiction a dream image cannot be lived, because while an author of fiction can propel his reader through any number of perversions and distortions of the mimetic tradition, he must do so in the name of some new perception of "reality." To abandon the category of the real altogether is to retreat into incantation, to cease to communicate. Hence the appropriateness of Raban's beetle-image: he has comfortably dropped below the threshold of the human. The actual story of Raban, as far as it goes, is a great deal more disorderly: transformations occur when not desired, and not when they are desired. The essential disorderliness of the relation between subject and object is the theme of "Description of a Struggle" (although a concept so orderly as "theme" can itself only be used provisionally). Neither the self nor its perceptions of the world can be relied on to remain stable or to change.

There is evidence that Kafka was uncertain how to proceed on the new level of ambiguity denoted by the term "evidently (offenbar)," for the two versions deviate significantly at this point. The narrator of the earlier version is embarrassed by his own behavior, attempts an overwrought psychological explanation (later deleted) of why he has been jumping around: "only in order not to appear helpless had I forced my merriment out of myself";[15] falls silent ("ich wurde stiller"), and experiences "shame" after slapping the acquaintance on the back. In the second version the narrator is more in control: he had "calculated," not just "expected," that his behavior would please the acquaintance, so no further explanation is necessary; his silence is similarly calculated ("Nun konnte auch ich stiller werden"), and the withdrawal of the hand is motivated by a sudden feeling that he doesn't understand the acquaintance's mental state. The two approaches then converge on the alienation he feels from the hand that has done the backslapping. Neither paragraph is satisfactory, because psychological linking matter seems lame and inappropriate next to the spontaneity of the two physical movements, the jumping around and the disposal of the hand. The divergences continue in the episode of the acquaintance's humming, and here the first version seems preferable, with its irregular shifting in the narrator's thoughts ("I found . . . I remembered . . . became a little gayer, one could almost say arrogant . . . imagined that I was out walking by myself").[16] One particular detail, the systematic contradiction apparent in the narrator's cheering up when he thinks of the liqueur he left behind, establishes the atmosphere precisely. In contrast the second version, by internalizing the narrator's thoughts and easing the transition from one to the next, makes him seem overly rational; the jolt comes anyway at the exclamatory conclusion of the paragraph, where the versions meet: "A way of life so natural that it borders on the excessive! (Eine in ihrer Natürlichkeit schon grenzenlose Lebensweise!)" Could the thought process Kafka has just sketched have concluded thus? The very posing of such a question suggests how tentative all judgments must be about "Description of a Struggle," a story that suspends all story-telling conventions. One could equally well argue that the narrator's thought sequence fits as just another piece into the overall collage of styles, without any tendency towards stratification of the narrator "as a person." The sequence offers support for Judith Ryan's differentiation between the narrators of the two versions: "Many reflections of the narrator, which in the first version occur in the form 'I found' or 'I thought,' are reproduced in the second version as interior monologue or 'erlebte Rede.' "[17] But her justifiable conclusion that the second version moves towards the limited, individual perspective of the mature works should not obscure the importance of fragmentation to the very conception of "Description": techniques like interior monologue are used to build up expectations in the reader which are then abruptly frustrated.

The differences between the versions are accentuated in the next paragraph, one of the most suggestive in the whole work. The versions begin more or less unanimously:

> But I wondered if it wouldn't be a good idea to turn down a side street; after all, I wasn't obliged to go on this walk with him. I could go home alone and no one could stop me.

They also end at the same point:

> But I was too timid to go away without a word and too weak to call to him out loud. So I stood still, leaned against the moonlit wall of a house, and waited.[18]

In these lines is prefigured the situation that is finally crystallized in the parable "Before the Law (Vor dem Gesetz)." From this early vantage point, untrammeled by the overtones of the "law," it can be seen how purely internal the obstacles to action are. It is a little like Zeno's paradox about the tortoise and Achilles; the only given element is the start the tortoise has over Achilles, and if one views this element in a certain way, using a system of a-priori fractions, one can prove that Achilles will never catch up with the tortoise. What is needed is a change in viewpoint. The Kafka hero, equipped with the logical system that proves he can never reach the tortoise, never tries to chase the tortoise or find another theory. Instead he spends his life seeking the flaw in the logic that dooms him to failure. Here the narrator is unable to go home because of the insurmountable preliminary of saying goodbye— or not saying goodbye. The fluid fragments of "personality" are suddenly dammed up. Into the void at the center of this irrationally "structured" consciousness there flood innumerable physiological trivia and social inhibitions, all of which seem to be "proofs that it's impossible to live (Beweise dessen, dass es unmöglich ist zu leben)," as the subtitle of the "Diversions" has it; the floodgate is then sealed by a simple phrase, like the doorkeeper's prohibition, and the protagonist, without any emotional transition, is in a position of total dependence, in possession of all his faculties except the awareness of freedom. What had previously been taken for granted ("no one could stop me") can no longer be conceived. After the acquaintance rejects the idea the narrator has no further thought of going home.

In between the passages quoted from this paragraph the narrator conjures up images of his home, and again the first version excels in evoking moods so swiftly contradictory that they are felt as simultaneities, just as, in "tree trunks in the snow," the illusion, the reality, and the illusion underlying reality coalesce into a single image. The narrator seeks out the comfortable stereotype in his furniture (the cliche aspect is underlined in the psychologically continuous second version), is overcome by the countervailing image of the place's depressing reality (suggested by the insistent, yet significantly "unreal" view of the floor as sloping in a mirror reflection), and decides to evade both present reality and the ambivalence of his room by doing the resolutely conventional thing and going to bed. This resolve is then suspended by the problem of saying goodbye described above, and the next paragraph presents, especially in the first version, the "struggle" of the title in its most concentrated form. While the acquaintance prattles about the maid's kiss the narrator is virtually tongue-tied; suddenly the indirections of both story and narrator, which have mirrored each other so closely, appear superseded by sentences suggesting calculation, tension and an urgent grasping at "freedom" as a source of identity for the narrator. Treating the acquaintance slightly paternally while counting on a drunkard's inattentiveness, he says: "Yes, you're right, we'll go home (Ja, Sie haben recht, wir werden nachhause gehn . . .)."[19] The bizarre sense of purposefulness persists through the common-sense chatter about work the next day, climaxing as the narrator holds out his hand to the acquaintance; in this gesture one senses a concentrated gamble for personal identity, analogous perhaps to Georg Bendemann's casually entering his father's room with a superficially innocuous letter. While the drama of "The Judgment" is of course absent, Kafka achieves here too a reversal, or rather dissolution, of roles in a few words: "But he smilingly echoed my turn of phrase: 'Yes, you're right, such a night shouldn't be wasted at home in bed.' "[20] The ambivalence of the "echo" ends the "struggle" as quickly as it had begun. Whether or not the acquaintance "intends" to defeat the narrator (and his words already have the impenetrable openness of Kafka's later style), his verbal repetition effectively eliminates all forward motion and reminds the reader that, in this theater of whim and artifice, no "drama" will ever be staged. The acquaintance follows his "victory" with a remark of unqualified emptiness ("Do you know what you are, you're funny") and he elicits this response: "I followed him without noticing it, absorbed by his statement."[21] Kafka has virtually canceled all the "characterization" up to this point: the narrator has forfeited all the elements of melancholy rootedness with which he began, and the acquaintance's seeming shrewdness has dissolved his image as a harmless philanderer. The final word, "statement," suggests the new level onto which the story is moving, one where words are autonomous, to be picked up or discarded by the imagination that hears them, but not to be sifted for anything they may reveal about "character."

Following the submergence of the concept of character, the reality-coordinate (the awareness that the "tree trunks" are rooted) is weakened progressively, though never finally eliminated. The narrator's consciousness is now free to follow whatever sequence of concepts or impressions it chooses: it comes to resemble a bouncing ball, touching regularly on reality but only in order to vault ever higher. So far I have quoted primarily from the first version, because its feverish perpetual motion better conveys the process of disintegration. But with the end of the narrator's attempt to hold his life together and the freeing of his fantasy, Kafka is more in need of the principle of opposition to prevent the story's becoming totally aimless. Here the cooler, more continuous style of the second version acquires a new effectiveness. For a connective logic has a peculiar piquancy (much exploited by absurdist writers of more recent years) when the reader can see its total unrelatedness to any "facts." Here are two passages, covering much the same ground, from the next paragraph:

> *First version:* I gazed at my acquaintance with loving eyes. In my mind I protected him against dangers, especially against rivals and jealous men. His life became dearer to me than my own. I found his face beautiful and I was proud of his success with women and I shared in the kisses he had received this evening from the two girls. Oh, what a gay evening this was! [My translation]

> *Second version:* Let's pray the girls won't spoil him! By all means let them kiss and hug him, that's their duty and his right,

> but they mustn't carry him off. After all, when they kiss him
> they also kiss me a little . . . . And supposing he falls down now
> or catches cold? Suppose some jealous man appears from the
> Postgasse and attacks him? What will happen to me? Am I to
> be just kicked out of the world? I'll believe that when I see it!
> No, he won't get rid of me. [Sterns's translation[22]]

One cannot argue that one passage is more "accurate" in its presentation of a human mind functioning; there is no entity "behind" the
words, demanding accuracy. But the obsessiveness of the thought-
sequence is suggested more vividly by the variety of initiatives and circular detailing of the second version; the more the narrator's thoughts
play about the acquaintance, the more the fundamental process of the
"tree trunks" passage is reinforced. The emphatic narrative voice belies
all unity of identity.

On a more general level, two further differences between the versions
become more striking towards the end of the section. First, in the later
version fewer emotions are actually attributed to the acquaintance, who
is presented instead through the physical impression he makes on the
narrator. The paradoxical variety opened up by the adoption of a single
perspective offers new scope to the playful anarchy of "Description."
The following sentence[23] brings out this shift clearly:

> *First version:* I didn't notice that he was surprised, when he
> bent over me sympathetically and stroked me with a soft hand.
> [My translation]

> *Second version:* I saw no signs of surprise as he bent down over
> me—lowering little more than his neck, exactly like a hyena—
> and stroked me with a soft hand. [Sterns's translation]

The restriction to physical impressions enlarges rather than narrows
the range of the narrator's reactions. A comparable expansion is noticeable in Kafka's method, in the later version, of employing an existing
categorical distinction, this time a literary one, to give shape to his
story through contrast. In the first version the speeches of both protagonists are embedded in the swirl of associations and reactions that constitutes the narrator's "thoughts": the premise is the total relativity of
experience, the mingling of the public and private domain. In the second
version Kafka presents the dialogues, both typographically and by
limiting the amount of accompanying comment, as functioning on a
separate plane from the narrator's stream of consciousness. Again there
is a foretaste of his later practice: one thinks of the self-contained, de-
batelike quality of some of the conversations in *The Castle*. Words in-

troduce a hierarchical element into the flux of experience, insisting on their public character, demanding analysis out of context, producing effects in the hearer that may be quite different from the speaker's intentions. We have already noted the intensified use of small phrases in the "struggle" paragraph of the first version, culminating in the transformation of "You're funny" into a "statement." In the more formalized dialogues of the second version surreal effects are achieved as the protagonists talk past each other, grasping only isolated phrases; especially amusing is the fate of the acquaintance's remark that it is 12:45 A.M., a comment that is dissected by the narrator and thrown back with the demand that it be retracted. The acquaintance responds: "But with pleasure, especially since a quarter to one passed long ago (Aber mit Vergnügen, umsomehr als dreiviertel längst vorüber ist)."

Both versions are concerned with the autonomous force of words, but whereas in the early version the narrator dissects both his own and the acquaintance's words in a kind of endless instant replay, the accent in the later version is on distance rather than proximity; the dialogues are set on a separate plane, often without introduction, intersecting with the comparatively smooth flow of the narrator's thoughts and casting it into relief. Thus when the two men are standing by the river and the narrator produces his "poetic memory" of the river (whether it is genuine or imaginary is unclear and unimportant), the speech is introduced thus in the first version: "Ashamed, I hastened to speak, in order to suppress my yawning (Beschämt beeilte ich mich zu reden, um mein Gähnen zu unterdrücken)." Even more significant, illustrating the close bond between an organized sequence of verbal images and the analytic alienation of "tree trunks in the snow," is his subsequent thought: "I spoke thus and tried painfully to discover behind my words love-stories with unusual situations"[24] (*erfinden* seems deliberately ambivalent, suggesting both "invent" and "discover"). The later, expanded, version of the speech, by contrast, begins with no more introduction than "I said (sagte ich)"; and Kafka sacrifices, at the end, the significant sentence just quoted in order to have the acquaintance simply interrupt the speech, having paid no attention whatever.

Still more striking is the way Kafka leads up to the narrator's fantasy that he is to be murdered. In the first version the narrator hysterically escalates a meditation about "happy people's ways (die Art der Glücklichen)" until it becomes the conviction that he is about to be attacked. In the second version this conviction appears as an established state of mind immediately after the dialogue about the time being 12:45 A.M.: "Obviously this was the time for the murder (Jetzt kam offenbar der Mord)." True, the narrator has been thinking of leaving during the dialogue, but the idea of murder comes from nowhere; Kafka has withdrawn a portion of the narrator's thought sequence in order to illustrate the dramatically unpredictable effects of language and gesture (the acquaintance has raised his right arm to listen to a tinkling chain on his cuff). Instead of the thought precipitating the deed (namely, flight), the cooler atmosphere of the second version then permits the narrator to debate with himself, in the manner of the better-known Kafka characters, the merits and demerits of the various courses of action, given death as the certain outcome.

The narrator's flight and ignominious collapse is really the only "event" of the entire story, in that the "outside world" is momentarily involved (Kafka did not develop the wounding at the end to the point of such contact). Following the analogy of the bouncing ball, the narrator's murder fantasy is a large leap out of the "real"; the depth to which he then appears to sink is thus nothing but a springboard for the final vault into the world of the "Diversions." Paradoxically, the "event" is the least real happening in the whole section: Kafka underlines this with the dry sequence of verbs describing the flight, culminating in the cinematic "I lay in the dark (ich lag im Dunkel)," a phrase strongly implying that the narrator has willed his own "failure," that the flight has not so much happened as been seen to happen. The representative of the world then pronounces a judgment on the incident with which all concerned, including the reader, must concur: "Nothing at all has happened (Es ist ja gar nichts geschehn)." This judgment, to the chagrin of the narrator, applies also to the tangible outcome of the flight, the pain in his knee. The acquaintance has no time for it, seeming to regard it as another irritating fancy of the narrator's. Not the outside world, not even the sensations of his own body, can generate an acknowledged identity for the narrator; and so the story's illogic develops a logical momentum of its own, as if the fictional act were filling the vacuum at its narrative source through an accelerated movement into an imagined world. I have perhaps phrased this too psychologistically —critical language, like that of literature, tends to impose its own categories. The point is that the "nothing" of the story's first part has engendered the "something" of the "Diversions," just as the earlier emotional "somethings" had dissolved in their own negations. And fragments of psychological connectedness persist, notably the bare power-relationship, the "struggle" that remains all the more latent for its failure to take concrete shape. The first "Diversion," in which the narrator rides on the acquaintance's back, foreshadows K.'s dream of success during the Bürgel chapter of *The Castle:* a vision of victory at the moment of defeat. It would be a mistake to press this further and interpret all the "Diversions" in psychological terms: the whole tendency of the story is towards the dismantling of such containers. At the same time it is true that the "Diversions" have their origin in the points of heightened "reality" in the consciousness of the narrator; the sensation of pain and the unsuccessful struggle with the acquaintance. Thus in the new atmosphere of relaxed fragmentation there hovers, as an unrealized and probably unrealizable opposite potentiality, the human longing for wholeness. The very title of the section suggests this; multiple proofs of the impossibility of living necessarily leave open the possibility that there is a way as yet untried, or at least not yet disproved.

The feeling of a single underlying voice, with the implied corollary that the variety of the world of illusion is itself an illusion, pervades the "Diversions." The category of Northrop Frye into which Kafka slips most easily is that of the ironic writer in the last stage of the mimetic cycle, through whose irony the outlines of a new myth can be discerned.[25] "Description of a Struggle" succinctly embodies this moment of literary history; no "reality" is immune from the author's ironic gaze. But the unique quality of Kafka's work resides in the nature of the myth he is seeking to articulate: this myth is presented most lucidly in the author's own statement quoted at the outset—the vision of a world in which the muddle of human perception is transmuted into an intense awareness of the two poles governing all perception, existence and nonexistence, *Etwas* and *Nichts*. But this is not a "usable," traditional kind of myth, not a myth of action that could bring order to human experience; it is rather a myth of perception, a myth that negates meaning in the very process of seeking it out. The substance of the action is not important in itself: Kafka gives the example of hammering as the kind of routine activity that needs to be transmuted. In other words, the experience of living is both intensified and emptied of normal meaning by its articulation as art and, vice versa, the terminology and perceptual level of a work of art must be identical with that of daily living, transmuted only by context.

The implications of this are far-reaching. Not only is a continuity apparent between the fragmented negations of "Description" and the tightly organized late stories, especially "Josefine, the Singer," the tale of a singer who sings less well than her audience, but it also seems likely that Kafka's purpose remained unchanged between these terminal points of his career. Periodizations like Sokel's, therefore, which seek to classify certain central works, according to their subject matter, as "punishment fantasies," are misleading. They suggest that Kafka dealt at one stage of his life with the "problem" of his family relations, and at another with the "problem" of being an artist. Whereas Kafka's unchanging, and frequently acknowledged, problem was one of presentation: how to organize the totality of his experience, including literary styles and topoi as well as the intricacies of his family life and the flatness of the office, in such a way that individual moments are both intensely "lived" and totally abstract, detached from their context by the process of writing. At the time of his most intense personal suffering, after the first dissolution of his engagement in July 1914, Kafka's diaries are indeed filled—but not with self-torture; he has time only for the banalities of hotel scenes and meals, Joycean "epiphanies" that he hopes to rescue from the flux because of the unusual intensity with which he is perceiving them.

Kafka did not again attempt, as in the "Diversions," to approach his mythical goal through the use of fantasy, preferring always to lay his groundwork, however briefly, in the often perverse logic of daily life. But the experiment helped to develop the structural principles that underpin his later works. The most prominent, as mentioned earlier, is the principle of antithesis, on which the Chinese-box effect of the first version is based. The tumbling moodiness of the narrator's initial fantasy is intersected by the statuesque, self-contained fat man, whose very fatness is of course in exaggerated contrast to the narrator, "a stick in perpetual motion (eine Stange in baumelnder Bewegung)." The fat man is in turn contrasted with the praying man, who is very like the narrator at one remove, with the shyness transformed into metaphysical anguish. The praying man's two basic experiences are equally antithetical. The miraculous normality of the sentence "I'm having my tea on the lawn (Ich jause im Grünen)" is a perfect example of Kafka's vision of the transmutation of reality through language (the magic of the single sentence, a legacy of Flaubert's, fascinated Kafka, as a comment in a letter to Felice of January 1913, quoting *L'Éducation sentimentale*, illustrates: " 'Elle avoua qu'elle désirait faire un tour à son bras, dans les rues!' What a sentence! What construction!").[26] Conversely, the expressionistic image of houses collapsing and people dying in the streets while society refuses to acknowledge anything (Kafka must surely be the first writer to have identified death as the modern obscenity) is the countervailing truth that expels the praying man from normality—and enables him, of course, to "glimpse" what others ignore. The principle of antithesis impels Kafka and his characters to lean on aspects of reality in the certainty that a totally different underside will emerge, the "nonexistence" that pervades all "existence." Thus the apparently ridiculous behavior of the praying man in attracting attention to his prayers is actually a desperate attempt to shore up his existence at the hours of dusk when his own and the world's disintegration become apparent. Similarly, the party from which the praying man is ejected is satirically presented, but only in part; both reader and praying man have the impression that everyone present has an identity which could easily be opened up. The girl whom the praying man first meets tells him: "for you the truth is too tiring (Die Wahrheit ist nämlich zu anstrengend für Sie)"; the host brings him the wrong clothes, which nevertheless fit him well; and collectively the guests regard his piano playing ironically: "Everyone seemed to know I couldn't play (Alle schienen zu wissen, dass ich es nicht konnte)." As if to test the impression that everyone has insights potentially superior to his own, the praying man then picks on an incapable drunk and attempts to provoke a response; the fantasies he spins are beginning to acquire a reality of their own, when the drunk responds after all. The response is minimal, but sufficient to suggest that even here there is a life beyond banality: "I don't even know if I have a brother-in-law at all (ich weiss ja nicht einmal, ob ich überhaupt einen Schwager habe . . .)."

The final striking example of antithetical movement, the self-wounding by the apparently so-secure acquaintance, emphasizes that there is a related modality in "Description of a Struggle," which could be termed "convergence." As antithesis is the technique whereby Kafka induces an effect of fragmentation without chaos, so convergence allows an insistent unity of tone to be apparent without reducing the number of characters to one. For as each scene progresses, the superficial oddities of each character tend to recede in significance, leaving the unmistakable voice of the "Kafka hero." In the case of the narrator and the praying man, the basic characteristics are divided between them, the narrator having the shyness, the incompetence, the submissiveness, while the praying man, seen mainly from the outside, is allowed the metaphysical insights and obsessions. Both combine a brooding introversion with a spontaneity inexplicable even to themselves. More surprising is the way the fat man tends to speak in similar tones. Great emphasis is placed on his monumental fatness; but the imagination is then strained by sentences like this, as he waits for the praying man: "At last I tiptoed to the door, slipped a coin to the blind beggar sitting there, and squeezed in beside him behind the open wing."[27] Similarly, he is presented initially as serene and self-controlled, but before he has even met the praying man he turns into the nervous Kafka-bachelor:

> I screwed up my mouth, this being the best preparation for resolute speech, and supported myself by standing on my right leg

while resting the left one on its toes, for this position as I have often experienced gives me a sense of stability.[28]

The convergence is completed when the acquaintance, who has maintained a separate voice throughout the first section, succumbs to the words "I am engaged (Ich bin verlobt)," and indeed the direction of this last section throws into relief the problematic quality of Kafka's writing at this stage. There is a neat symmetry in the turning of the tables in the struggle, the banality of "I am engaged" trumping that of "You're funny"; one can also argue that the theme of fragmentation is enhanced by the breakup of the only remaining "character." But with the end of the "struggle," there is really an end to the story's vitality: the narrator cannot in any meaningful sense "win," and without his mental dependence on the at least partially unknown quantity of the acquaintance, his thoughts are just uninteresting. It is no accident that the story ends as a fragment. For all its fertility, the basically circular movement of its structure prevents it from gaining fictional life. The technique of antithesis opens up every human mind; that of convergence dictates that what emerges is something very like the angst and insecurity of the basic Kafka-character, whereupon the antithetical impulse shifts to a new and apparently exotic figure and the process begins again. The result is a strange society of outsiders sustained only by the hope of finding an "insider"; but the whole movement of the story precludes this possibility—in this world there *cannot* be anyone who will say "I'm having my tea on the lawn (Ich jause im Grünen)" without irony. Ultimately openness becomes weightlessness. "Description of a Struggle" shows Kafka free of all stylistic inhibitions and equipped with the essential themes and techniques of his later works. After this experiment in a fiction that resists the characteristics of fiction and so finally forfeits its vitality, Kafka will need to retrench on two basic points: his all-pervading personal voice must be concentrated in a single continuous consciousness, and this consciousness must be differentiated from all the subsidiary characters, who will therefore withdraw from the realm of the known into that of the potential. Technically his later work thus has more affinities with the fiction of the past, but one convention is never used: the omniscience of the narrator. The permanent gain from "Description of a Struggle" is the blurring of the line between fantasy and reality, the incorporation of the mind's own categories into the subject matter of fiction. Kafka's heroes never "know" more than the other characters, and often much less.

2   Open Structure: "The Stoker"

The difficulties of dating the "fragment," "The Stoker," and the novel *America* (*Der Verschollene*) of which it was to form the first chapter, are set out by Pasley and Wagenbach in the *Kafka-Symposion*.[1] My interest here is in the date of conception and initial work on the novel: the letter to Felice of 9–10 March 1913 refers to "about 200 pages of an utterly useless version of the story, written in the winter and spring of last year,"[2] thus dating the early stages of the work at winter-spring 1911–1912. This is confirmed by a diary entry of 9 May 1912 implying prolonged involvement in the novel. The conception of *America*, as opposed to any kind of final version, thus predates "The Judgment" by nearly a year. Of course, this does not bring it at all close in time to "Description of a Struggle" (1904–5) and, in order to show that "The Stoker," the only part of the work Kafka deemed publishable, is a kind of artistic "second stage" in his development, I must rest my case solely on internal analysis.

The central question raised by "The Stoker" involves the "reliability" of the world portrayed. Jörgen Kobs rejects the argument of Jörg Thalmann that the novel *America* represents a conscious extension of naturalism; Kobs shows that the destructive dialectic between "minuteness" and "uncertainty" pervades the texture quite as strongly here as in the later novels. But while conceding that the "objectivity" of Kafka's style is illusory, one retains a strong sense that Kafka's purpose here is different: after all, in a diary entry for 8 October 1917 he referred to "The Stoker" as a "sheer imitation of Dickens."[3] The phrase gives us a clue; Kafka was not "continuing" a tradition, he was "imitating" a style he already regarded as historical. "The Stoker" is a restaging of a realistic story, literally a reenactment of the narrative enterprise in the theater of the hero's mind. This explains why Karl Rossmann has virtually no "private" characteristics, why he seems defined by his urge to restore "order" in his world. This urge was, precisely, Kafka's own, which he could only articulate through a surrogate hero. The principle of antithesis has found a complete expression in Karl: his reactions are so "simple," so devoid of background and ulterior motives, because the role he is acting out is the most complex conceivable—that of the novelist endeavoring to create a world. Kobs takes full account of Karl's "rage for order," but his explanation is ultimately circular.

"If Karl Rossmann endeavors to assign a fixed position to everyone present, if he imposes spatial coordinates on the people around him— or better, if he transfixes them like insects at a specified location—then the motive of his striving towards peace and 'overview' is again revealed as the unconditional claim to dominance of his subjectivity."[4] This does not answer the question posed by Karl's status as a fictional character: *why* does Karl seek to impose his subjectivity on events? The rhythm may be the same as that of the later novels, but the hero's struggle for identity has a different focus. The term "open structure" is intended as a definition of the fiction generated by Karl's consciousness. Precisely, the "openness" that ultimately vitiated "Description of a Struggle" is transformed into a "structure"; the game of fusing literary styles has become the task of creating a single style.

Kafka's description of Rossmann, in a diary entry of 30 September 1915, as "the innocent . . . more pushed aside than struck down (der Schuldlose . . . mehr zur Seite geschoben als niedergeschlagen),"[5] suggests the necessary location of the hero in an open structure. Karl is easily pushed aside because standing aside is his basic posture; his attempt to define himself in terms of the order of the world is "selfless," when contrasted with the thrust of later Kafka heroes. Karl's "self" can only exist if the values of the Dickensian novel can be verified as holding together the world outside himself: such values as justice, functioning social relations, consistency of character, at the very least a logical connection between happenings. Karl employs a variety of strategies, as Kobs shows: he intervenes, he observes, he rationalizes. But this very variety is at odds with the essential simplicity implied in his posture as narrator of an "objective" story. Gradually it becomes clear that he is creating, not a realistic story, but an almost mathematical inversion of such a story: Karl, like the sorcerer's apprentice, finds that his tools cannot be controlled, that they generate a world that appears "realistic" but systematically eludes the continuous meaning that could transform appearance into structure. This world "opens out"; the necessity of the hero's voice produces only contingency, a parataxis of events leading nowhere. That "The Stoker" is nevertheless clearly felt to be a structure is due entirely to the exactly parallel movement of Karl's consciousness. At the beginning we see him alone and jostled yet entirely at one with his world. At the end he has found a place of his own in the world—and feels that he has lost everything of importance. But so long as Karl pursues the mirage of ordered realism, his existence will continue and the "unity" of his enterprise will be guaranteed by the symmetrically unfulfilled duality of self and world.

Karl emerges, as it were, from anonymity. The first sentence endows him with a set of facts that constitute a past, but the principle of antithesis works immediately to ensure that this recitation, far from "explaining" Karl, effectively cuts him off from everything but the present moment. By compressing into a single sentence information appropriate to a more relaxed mode of narration, Kafka has coined his own convention: the hero who is artificially close to his immediate surroundings, untrammeled by memory, referring his reactions only to the abstractions of common sense. In *The Trial* and *The Castle* the protagonist is also close to events in this way, but there the method underlines the extreme disparity between a situation and his mental analysis of it. Here, on the other hand, Karl begins in harmony with (one might almost say, indistinguishable from) his circumstances, and has no desire to assert an independent existence. Fundamentally passive, his "initiatives" are really reactions, efforts to restore the order of the world that he feels has been violated. His being alone and this concern for order, which is no more than the desire to assent to the status quo, are Karl's only identifying features. In the second paragraph he admires the size of the Statue of Liberty, heedless of the fact that he is being shoved against the railings by the crowd. If he can see the world outside in good order, he will not complain. Untroubled by countercurrents, he is to enter a life of orderly obscurity: Kafka underlines this point in the course of the story by drawing attention to phenomena, like the size of the ship and the movement of the sea, that Karl had not noticed during the voyage, but which strike him now. Clearly, if Karl's world had not shifted out of order, his attempt to "recreate" that world in Dickensian terms would never have come to seem necessary.

But the world does shift. As in many of Kafka's later works, a small detail, here the forgetting of the umbrella, causes the world with which the hero is familiar suddenly to become strange. In an open structure, however, as Pasley stresses,[6] this detail does not at once appear inevitable, fateful, symbolic; rather, like the other details in the story it retains a degree of arbitrariness, of autonomy. It is precisely the need to combat this arbitrariness that gives Karl his literary existence; should he manage to impose order on the world, he would achieve an "identity" —which would instantly dissolve together with his narrative function.

Frank Kermode has said: "We may call books fictive models of the temporal world. They will be humanly serviceable as models only if they pay adequate respect to what we think of as 'real' time, the chronicity of the waking moment."[7] If Kafka has proved to be an eminently "serviceable" writer in the modern world, this is in part because of his unique ability to maintain the reader's belief in the "reality" of his fictions while implying forcefully that this reality is only the tip of an iceberg. It cannot be directly known, because it is not "known" to the central character: the events are both "something" and "nothing," perceived all the more intensely because they are the only guarantee, however enigmatic, of the hero's precarious existence. In this story both Karl Rossmann and his world come into being on the basis of mutual destruction. Karl only perceives the world as a system at the point when it is ceasing to function as such, when causality is being subtly transformed into contingency. This process is vividly presented in the third paragraph, which relates a perfectly "normal" series of occurrences while subtly overextending them so that there is no doubt about their impact on Karl's mind. There is an immediate explanation for the closing-off of the corridor; nevertheless it is "for the first time." It is entirely probable that he would wander through a passenger lounge in search of the right exit—but what he notices is the deserted writing table suggestive of a mind becoming rapidly aware of its own aloneness. Naturally everyone is on deck; but the odd fact that he meets absolutely no one allows the noise of their feet to become an image heightening Karl's feeling of having wandered into the underworld. And the engines are just being turned off; normal enough, yet Karl's mind moves now on the level of imagery and hears them as "breathings," the expiration of the familiar world. This accumulation of detail erects an antithetical metaphor parallel to the surface events, so that when Kafka writes "a little door by which he had chanced to stop" the reader, without having to think forward to the parable "Before the Law," instinctively translates the phrase as "a door destined for Karl."

Karl is semihysterical when he bangs on the door: it is immediately clear that the reader will be unable to distinguish between "external" and "internal" loss of order. Kafka, maintaining Karl's perspective, does not describe the hysteria, since Karl himself is not fully conscious of it, but it emerges through the stoker's addressing him as a "madman," "hammering" rather than knocking. The ironic point is that though Karl seeks reunion with the "normal" world, the displacement of reality he has experienced makes him want something more vividly reassuring, more archetypal—in a word, a sign. The stoker's apparent normality is no longer enough for Karl, as his odd question about the man's nationality underlines. Kafka is careful to explain this, to maintain the naturalistic texture. But he allows Karl's state out into the open with the thought: "But it's now we were speaking about (Es handelt sich doch um jetzt)"; it is not, of course, a question of "now," but of the stoker's natural dislike of people talking to him from the doorway. The thought expresses, rather, Karl's sense that "now" is unlike anything he has known before. The thought is submerged again in the practical question of Karl's trunk. Or rather, for the stoker it is practical; for Karl it immediately goes deeper, reinforcing his conviction of being lost. When the stoker utters the word "alone," Karl's reaction reveals the dissonance within: " 'Perhaps I should join up with this man,' the thought came into Karl's head. 'Where am I likely to find a better friend?' "[8] The simultaneous acceleration and depersonalization implicit in "came into Karl's head" reminds one of "The Judgment": in both cases the issue suddenly seems to the hero to be his own survival, although they have reached the point from opposite directions, Georg struggling to avoid extinction, Karl forced out of anonymity into the task of existence.

Kafka heightens the movement of panic in Karl's mind with the apparently innocent phrase: "looking round for the way out (. . . und sah sich um, wie er hinauskommen könnte)." When one remembers that Karl has just decided to cling to the stoker as a friend, these words suggest the urge to shed the burden of consciousness by whatever means, to regain a collectivity that now seems instinctual. The rough physical response of the stoker is thus a precisely symmetrical move, propelling Karl back into the recreative role he is seeking to evade. The stoker's action brings to an end the movement towards disintegration within Karl: "exasperation" is already a less instinctual response. But the stoker's revelation of his function at once generates a contrasting impulse in Karl, a thrust towards reintegration that sets his basic course for the remainder of the story. The irrationality of his joy at the stoker's remark is underlined by the self-alienated "as if" which Kafka has pointed toward in "Description of a Struggle": "as if this surpassed all his expectations (als überstiege das alle Erwartungen)."

Although Karl is not dependent on the stoker the way the narrator succumbs to the acquaintance in "Description," there are suggestive parallels. In the earlier work the struggle with the acquaintance completed the fragmentation of the narrator's already fragile identity. Here the motif of struggle is involved in a drive towards reintegration; in alliance with the stoker cast as "insider" Karl will reimpose order through acceptance of his own role as authorial "outsider." The general critical assumption that Karl is innocent and spontaneous in his advocacy of the stoker's cause is not borne out by the text. True, Karl is an "experimental" character in his freedom from the self-destructive obsessions of the other two of Kafka's "sons," Georg Bendemann and Gregor Samsa. At the same time, the very neutrality of his persona at the beginning of the story generates its own distortions of perspective. The slightest loss of continuity or gain in complexity provokes an exaggerated reaction in Karl as he strives to impose the lucidity of Dickensian fiction on his surroundings. Karl may not have to justify himself, as so many of Kafka's characters do, but he is compelled to seek an "identity" through justification of the world.

In "Description of a Struggle," as we saw, Kafka adopts the viewpoint of several characters, with the result that they all tend to sound alike. In "The Stoker" the open structure and the single perspective are designed to exclude convergence; but Kafka uses just enough of it to sharpen the pressure on his central character. The stoker is clearly and independently characterized, but just as Karl has assigned him the role of life-model, with himself as eager apprentice, the stoker refuses his role in radically ambivalent terminology: "I don't suppose you're thinking seriously of being a stoker, but that's just the time when you're most likely to turn into one."[9] The developing situation has once again been upset: the man whose function is so symbolically "inside" society is after all an "outsider." Instead of entering the world with the stoker as master and himself as apprentice, Karl finds himself called upon to make an alliance of the oppressed, as the stoker embraces and elaborates on the hero's unthinking cliché: "Anyway, people here have a prejudice against foreigners (Überhaupt ist man hier gegen Fremde so eingenommen . . .)."

While the stoker speaks, Kafka suggests the renewed turmoil in Karl only by two modifying words: "confused" and "excitedly" ("wirr" and "aufgeregt"), and when the stoker ceases speaking, Kafka presents Karl's new state of mind symbolically: "He had almost lost the feeling that he was on the uncertain boards of a ship, beside the coast of an unknown continent, so much at home did he feel here in the stoker's bunk."[10] With almost mathematical symmetry Kafka situates Karl's illusion of ordered unity at the point where the quest for order is definitively revealed as imposing ceaseless duality and tension. Karl's earlier sense of relief at learning the stoker's function has established an irresistible momentum, and the stoker's story presents him with the unassailable value of "justice" with which to underpin his relationship with the world. From this point there is no going back, as Karl's gloomy meditation following the stoker's rejection of his advice makes clear. The trunk, eloquently neutral symbol of his anonymity (he was what he owned) before the loss of his umbrella, now seems impossibly far away. He can no longer understand his own behavior in regard to the trunk; his mind wanders helplessly around the immediate past; without the stoker nothing now fits together, and the ultimate fragmentation of sleep is his only recourse. The stoker then takes the initiative and Karl resumes the task he cannot now evade: recreating an ordered world around the stoker as centerpiece. The stoker's "story," for all its banality, has the minimal shape which Karl sees as guaranteeing fictional truth. An important stage in this movement is Karl's pause by the window of the administration cabin; contemplating the ceaseless motion of sea, ships, and traffic in New York harbor, Karl again indulges the illusion of achieved order: "Yes, in this room one realized where one was (Ja, in diesem Zimmer wusste man, wo man war)." The phrase is significant because Karl could presumably have had the same view from any number of portholes. The words reflect Karl's longing to identify with the ship's establishment; as bona fide insiders, it is in their power to end his "story," thereby simultaneously affirming his identity as creator and restoring his anonymity.

Thalmann, rejecting the common notion that we are witnessing the drama of individuals fighting a "corrupt world order," states the situation precisely:

> Even on close examination of the text we find no explicit statement, no hint that, in the quarrel with Chief Engineer Schubal, justice is on the side of the stoker.[11]

This uncertainty reflects no more than the truism that there are two sides to every argument about human rights and values. But Karl is concerned, not with facts but with his own authorial imperative to restore "order" in the world. And it is this clear-cut objective that leads to the deepest ambivalence. If there already is a stable order in the world (and Karl's sense of fulfillment by the window indicates his instinctive assumption that there is), then the stoker's situation need only be brought to the attention of the powers that be for rectification to be automatic; but if, as the shape of Karl's "story" prescribes, the world order has been crippled by the historic injustice done to the stoker, an uncompromising crusade on the stoker's behalf is required. The paradox of Karl's posture can only be heightened as he intervenes on behalf of his own fiction. Just as there was an element of excess and of surprise at himself in his first identification with the stoker (indicated by the phrase "as if this surpassed all his expectations"), so the emphatic nature of his first speech on the stoker's behalf has a self-canceling effect. Karl observes himself speaking and notes that he is distorting his own role in order to make the case clear-cut; what has not reached the threshold of his consciousness is that the banal heroics of his words are bound to create an awkward atmosphere for the stoker in presenting his case to people who know the facts. It is as if Karl is testing the hypothesis that an injustice has been done at the very moment when he is supposedly acting on the truth of that hypothesis. His state of mind is revealed in the curious sentence: "Everything now depended on the stoker's behavior, for about the justice of his case Karl had no doubt whatever."[12] If the ship's officers are sensitive to injustice, presumably they will overlook any awkwardness on the stoker's part; if they are not sensitive, or are involved in a conspiracy to keep the stoker down, then diplomatic skill will be of no avail. What Karl means by "everything" is that he is willing the stoker to achieve the impossible: express both outrage against injustice and fundamental allegiance to the existing order in such a way that all rifts are healed.

Two related questions arise. Can the passage quoted be unambiguously construed as Karl's thought? And, if my interpretation is correct, can one say that Karl is "exploiting" the stoker? Somewhat as in "The Judgment" (though to very different effect), Kafka has constructed a story in two parts: in the first section (inside the stoker's cabin), the essential elements are established—the primacy of Karl's perspective and his acceptance of his task as "author" of the stoker's story. In the second part (the scene with the officers) a very different atmosphere prevails, with much action and contention, a struggle of tactics and power groupings. But upon closer examination virtually nothing happens (in "The Judgment"'s second part it is the other way round, conversational banalities being used as masks and weapons in an existential conflict). Karl's only volitional impact on the scene is accomplished by his initial speech. Though it may have presented the stoker in an exaggerated light, it does him no tangible harm—and it brings about a hearing when otherwise none might have occurred. The doubts one has about the speech, as outlined above, do not concern the public realm of possible gains or losses for the stoker, but the ambivalent state of mind revealed by Karl's words. The story's second part, in other words, is as exclusively concerned with Karl's mind as the first; the difference lies in the author's structural technique. In the first part, where Karl's mental state *is* the plot, Kafka employs a technique of antithesis, showing both Karl's increasing clarity concerning his fiction-making task and, in counterpoint, the growing opaqueness, elusiveness of the material to which he is committed. In the second part the stoker's complaint and the senator's intervention generate all the "events," and Kafka, having established the functionality of Karl's perspective, is free to present Karl's mind with a kind of detached intensity. Events occur and Karl is intimately involved in them—but, apart from his first initiative, he does not cause them. Thus the reader witnesses the bare events, the endless encrustations added to them by Karl's mind—and additional perspectives, notably the stoker's, that counteract Karl's suppositions even as he is formulating them.

What Kafka has risked here is an extreme loosening of the single perspective, not quite to the point where the reader protests, "Karl couldn't have known that" or "A teenager couldn't have thought that," but to the point where both these reactions would be justified if Kafka had not already so thoroughly established the primacy of Karl's perspective. Two examples: in addition to frequent use of the neutral "one" (*man*) to provide impressions, there is a passage, on Schubal's supposed tactics, that far exceeds the reasoning power we have become accustomed to in Karl; and the paragraph near the end, beginning "And yet the stoker seemed to have abandoned hope (Und trotzdem schien der Heizer nichts mehr für sich zu hoffen)" presents a sequence of thoughts that could hardly have been deduced from the stoker's facial expression. And yet the introductory "seemed" indicates that Kafka is not actually changing perspective. Wolfgang Jahn, perhaps too paradoxically, regards the single perspective as actually reinforced by this passage:

> In truth . . . these are Karl's thoughts; for Karl has for a moment transformed himself, as it were, into the stoker and now registers the hopelessness of the situation from the latter's presumed perspective. The unity of perspective is not thereby shattered—on the contrary, for the identification exists only in Karl's imagination. The author, by omitting to specify the imagined identification as such, dissolves narrative distance altogether and creates a complete oneness in the mental processes.[13]

Similarly, the excited language of Karl's thoughts about Schubal emphasizes that Karl's personality is very much a part of these logical imaginings. Kafka has broadened Karl's perspective to include both a quest, through a form of inductive logic, for the implications of human actions, and a kind of behavioral psychology that "explains," as far as is necessary, the feelings of other people.

We are now in a position to answer the questions raised earlier. The logical form of the statement "Everything now depended on the stoker's behavior (Jetzt hing alles vom Benehmen des Heizers ab)" suggests the merging of Karl's viewpoint with a less private way of thinking, but this only underlines the widening scope of Karl's fiction making, the need to include all possible meanings in the formulation of a "realistic" myth. And Karl does indeed "exploit" the stoker—as an artist exploits his material. Karl functions on a different plane from the stoker's "real" concerns. It makes no sense to talk of hidden motives in a character wholly defined by the "external" events to which he is committed. Kafka's "imitation" of Dickens veers rather towards the Homeric epic, with its hero's self-definition in terms of surface and narrative function.

Karl's "personality" is intensified rather than diluted by this use of flexibility in perspective. Kafka is able to dramatize the dichotomy between his commitment to the stoker's story and his counter-movement towards anonymity, by variously weighting the symbolic objects on which his consciousness seizes. Leaving the linear norms of the narrative mode far behind him, Kafka conveys intensities of both involvement and detachment within a single unemphatic sentence. The seeds of Karl's self-fragmentation appear even as the stoker is launching his plea:

> At this point Karl fixed his eyes on the Captain and stared at him with earnest deference, as if they had been colleagues, to keep him from being influenced against the stoker by the man's awkward way of expressing himself.[14]

The significant phrase is "as if they had been colleagues": even as Karl pours his concentration into support for the stoker, he is also thrusting toward a symmetrical "end" to the story—which can only come from those who are detached from or hostile to the stoker and find him "awkward." Not surprisingly, Karl's concentration is dissipated in the general "dispersion of interest" (*Zerstreuung*); as the officers return to their tasks, his gaze returns to the scene at the window which had originally induced a sense of harmony with the world: the scene is now as unsettled—"a movement without end"—as Karl's own vacillating purpose. Thrusting himself back into the stoker's cause, Karl intervenes—but his words are very different from those of his first speech: patronizing rather than sympathetic, they reflect a fictive reinforcement of the captain's position, going beyond the merely tactical. By dwelling on the speech's effect on the stoker, Kafka illuminates Karl's loss of control over his enterprise at the moment when his myth making is gathering momentum. When the stoker turns on Karl, neither Karl nor the reader really feels his act to be capricious: "But the stoker mistook the action, feeling, no doubt, that Karl was nursing some secret reproach against him"[15]—the subtle expansion of perspective allows the truth to be presented as if in a mirror; these are Karl's impressions of the stoker's instinctive understanding of where Karl's sponsorship has led him. The culminating antithesis of this series is Karl's despairing negation of his own allegiance to order, his brief vision of the possibility of chaos through electrical sabotage.

With the change in Karl's status after the senator's intervention, his state of mind changes too—but not towards the longed-for, and now freely offered, harmony with the status quo. At the beginning of the scene he had, as it were, committed his existence to the fictional shaping of the present moment, by placing his passport on the officer's desk. But when the bare facts of his past are reanimated as an "identity," when anonymity is re-presented as individuality, the subsequent recognition scene, to use Clemens Heselhaus's term, belongs indeed to a "fairy tale in reverse" (*Antimärchen*).[16] The oscillating perspective is suddenly frozen. Karl feels entirely alienated from the events of his past that are spread before him; defining himself by the contours of the present, he cannot see the relevance of such artificial "inwardness," such a complacent certification of the Bildungsroman. His life is now "whole," but its consistency is without meaning, a set of fragmented feelings without function. A ghastly formality becomes the all-pervading reality. Karl shakes hands with Schubal; the "aesthetic" function of this gesture, to be discussed further in the context of *The Trial*, lies in its surface conclusiveness. Karl seeks some kind of finale to a story which, following its antithetical rhythm, has been totally drained of meaning by Karl's "reintegration" and consequent loss of authorial perspective (the fundamental, if unrealized, desirability of the outsider's posture will be a central motif in our discussion of *The Castle*):

> "Except that I'm afraid I've lost my box"—and with that he remembered all that had happened and all that remained to be done, and he looked around him and saw the others still in the same places, silent with respect and surprise, their eyes fixed upon him.[17]

Rigidity pervades the final scene with the stoker, Karl's tears notwithstanding. Karl merely reiterates, as if in search of a lost sensation, the unresolved elements of his relationship with the stoker: the reproach that the stoker's militancy was insufficient to overcome injustice and reintegrate the world—and the renewed invocation of a cause from which he is now, physically as well as mentally, withdrawing. The word "playfully" (*spielend*), describing Karl's handshake with the stoker, brings to mind the "playful slowness (spielerische Langsamkeit)"[18] with which Georg Bendemann seals a letter in the first paragraph of "The Judgment." The atmosphere of the two passages is very different, but in both there is a hint at the growing importance of "play" as a mode of characterization in Kafka's work. The gestures express an empty mastery, self-control in a vacuum.

In the open structure the reader witnesses, simultaneously, Karl's failure to impose his own notion of a "story" on the world—and the emergence of a very different "story" from Karl's assumption of an authorial role. If it seems that this sentence could be transferred to "The Burrow," that is no accident; in his last phase Kafka used several variants of the open structure. There, as here, the hero sponsors the shape of his world and is then trapped, his function called into question by the ironic open-endedness of his own creation: one feels Karl's story could develop in many different directions simply by the principle of antithesis, the development of the countertendencies that are present in any situation, and which his adopted role will force into the open. In the final sentences of "The Stoker," even as Karl is subjectively rounding out the story with a "dramatic" flood of tears conveying personal loss, he is also comparing the stoker with his uncle—and the uncle is avoiding his gaze. The situation is thus open-ended, and the antithetical elements in the uncle's character duly emerge in the next chapter, canceling the illusion of stasis at the close of "The Stoker."

The open structure is therefore paratactic, fulfilling Staiger's primary definition of "the epic." Martin Walser's terminology is very appropriate when, speaking of *America* as a whole, he asks, "Does this series of events bear within it the seeds of a finite development and recapitulation, or is a process of infinite addition possible?" and answers decisively in the latter sense:

> Either Karl must give up his own idea of order and therewith the very roots of his existence, or he will be negated again and again by the counterorder which, for its part, cannot change under any circumstances.[19]

Walser is here describing a basic dialectic which he perceives in all three of Kafka's novels, whereby the hero's struggles for self-assertion are preordained to failure and are continually renewed. Karl Rossmann, as we have seen, fits the pattern only partially, for his basic movement is towards the restitution of order rather than self-assertion. Nevertheless, Walser's description of an endlessly renewed and shifting interaction between Karl and his environment is an accurate characterization of the open structure. The reason I prefer the term "antithesis" to Walser's *Aufhebung* is that it is in no sense existential and carries no connotations of struggle. Antithesis, the simultaneity of illusion and "reality" crystallized in the image in the "tree trunks in the snow," underlies the individual perceptions from which a conception of the world is built up. Applied to a sequence of occurrences in fictional time, it throws earlier events into relief by canceling their meaning for a subsequent point in time. Karl views his behavior in guarding the trunk during the voyage with an analytic intensity because he no longer understands his own purpose; he becomes all the more attached to the stoker because the latter is not the "insider" he had imagined; he presses the stoker's cause with a vehemence proportionate to his declining identification with it. The principle of antithesis thus tends to replace the linearity of fiction with a form of relativity: each event is provisional. The more definitive it seems (e.g., the senator's intervention), the more certainly is its meaning undermined. As each event also modifies preceding events, nothing is lost to view, and nothing remains fixed. Karl's memory of his seduction dominates him exclusively—for a while, as does his determination to work for the stoker's cause. The reader is not tempted to organize the priorities in Karl's mind, for the struggle to establish priorities is synonymous with his drive towards a fictional order—a struggle doomed by the sheer successiveness of experience. Each impression is crucially important to Karl, only to be temporarily effaced by an entirely different one. By accelerating the sequence of perceptions to the point of virtual simultaneity, Kafka has brought into focus both the insistent temptation and the ultimate impossibility of the "realistic story."

The difficulty of applying an essentially static, or circular, perceptual mode to the inherent linearity of fiction was apparent to Kafka at the outset of his work on *America*. A paradox central to the thought of this most dialectical of writers was his dislike of his own antitheses, with their insistent drive towards autonomy:

> My repugnance for antitheses is certain. They are unexpected, but do not surprise, for they have always been there; if they were unconscious, it was at the very edge of consciousness. They make for thoroughness, fullness, completeness, but only like a figure on the "wheel of life"; we have chased our little

idea around the circle. They are as undifferentiated as they are different, they grow under one's hand as though bloated by water, beginning with the prospect of infinity, they always end up in the same medium size. (20 November 1911)[20]

There is in fact a mechanical quality, a "medium size," about the fiction generated by Karl Rossmann. Because he is "without background," defined solely in terms of his immediate experience, a paradoxical sameness is built into the very unpredictability of events. Precisely because there is no limit to the variety of Karl's potential experience, the texture gradually becomes dominated by the strict rhythm of his relationship to that experience. The use of antithesis is fundamental to Kafka's style, and its quality of rigidity will only be exorcised when it becomes thematic; at the point when Kafka's heroes themselves become partially or intermittently (but never fully) aware of the displacement imposed on the world by their subjective rhythms, then the essentially combative dimension of the narrative theater will have been achieved.

3 "The Urban World":
The Experience of the Theater

If we are to demonstrate systematically (as opposed to impressionistically) the importance of the theater for Kafka's works, we must study what he has left us of his literary workshop in the decisive years 1911–12, reaching back before the conception of *America*. That he was anxiously seeking alternative fictional modes is evident from a fragment entitled "The Urban World [Die städtische Welt]," printed in his diary between the entries of 21 February and 26 March 1911.[1] This is in one sense a sketch for "The Judgment": Kafka specifically mentions it in his list of "influences" contained in the ecstatic diary entry about the writing of "The Judgment." But it is also an interesting stylistic experiment.

The central character, Oskar M., is instantly recognizable as the "Kafka hero," but is denied the most central attribute of later Kafka heroes, the controlling perspective. Not that any other perspective is offered; but the "reactions" of Oskar are strictly behavioristic and the bulk of the fragment is a dialogue with the father in which the linking matter is as purely external as possible, like stage directions. The first paragraph is worth quoting in full for the curiously independent positioning of the "narrator":

> Oskar M., an older student—if one looked at him closely one was frightened by his eyes—stopped short in the middle of a snowstorm on an empty square one winter afternoon, in his winter clothes with his winter coat, over it a shawl around his neck and a fur cap on his head. His eyes blinked reflectively.

He was so lost in thought that once he took off his cap and stroked his face with its curly fur. Finally he seemed to have come to a conclusion and turned with a dancing movement onto his homeward path.[2]

The last sentence is reminiscent of "Description of a Struggle," but there the dissociation of comprehension from action occurs within the framework of a first-person narration: "Hardly were we outside when I evidently began to feel very gay (Kaum waren wir ins Freie getreten als ich offenbar in grosse Munterkeit geriet)." Here the narrator is like a spectator in the theater, recording only the striking details of a scene. The ensuing dialogue strengthens this theatrical impression: it reads like a systematic blending of cliché-speech, high-sounding sentiments that fit the "roles" of a father and a son, with a needling exploitation by both sides of the peculiarities of the son's position. In this "struggle" the contestants use the conventions of family roles as a shield, the son's assertions of individuality as a sword. Of course, the son loses and saves himself by flight.

This use of the theatrical mode, the attempt to portray the inner life solely through what comes to the surface in the shape of speech and gesture, seems at first like a literal implementation of Kafka's later dictum:

One cannot express what one is, for that *is* precisely what one is; one can communicate only what one is not, that is, the lie. Only in the chorus there may be a certain truth.[3]

"The Urban World" does indeed employ a "choral" mode, attempting to build a "true" portrait of Oskar through an accumulation of his "lies," unmodulated by his self-interested perspective.

But "The Urban World" remains an unfocused curiosity, failing to communicate the powerful emotions that have obviously been poured into it. It suffers, in fact, from a weakness discussed in connection with "Description of a Struggle": the lack of a controlling "voice" to which the reader can relate all statements made. As "Description" loses impetus by the dismantling of the narrator's "character," so here the complementary difficulty is apparent: it does not seem possible to reconstruct Oskar's character from a sequence of enigmatic statements and gestures—but neither can the reader renounce the idea of "character" altogether. Kafka is asking the reader to experience a series of "provisional" realities: each speech of Oskar is related to the immediate juncture of the struggle with the father, rather than to earlier speeches of Oskar himself. Lämmert warns that, if literature can be legitimately seen as a "conversation" with the reader, then the bare sequence of "lies" such as we find in "The Urban World" violates the premise of the literary conversation:

> Through the artistic shaping of language every detail acquires a special stamp and resonance: a certain connectedness, which prevents the reader or listener from regarding it only as a step towards the next detail and abandoning it as a "partial experience" as soon as the next detail is reached.[4]

Lämmert also stresses the analogy between the reading of fiction and the human experience of living in time, and this analogy must have helped to move Kafka away from the "scenic" method of "The Urban World." Kafka's sense of the human predicament cannot be confined to the framework of a "situation" like the struggle with the father; moreover, the experience of time is fundamental to Kafka's insights into that predicament.

Of the many passages in the diaries where Kafka evokes the atrophied misery of the bachelor's life, none is more striking than that written on 14 November 1911, concluding thus:

> This is all true, but it is easy to make the error of unfolding future sufferings so far in front of one that one's eye must pass beyond them and never again return, while in reality, both today and later, one will stand with a palpable body and a real head, a real forehead that is, for smiting on with one's hand.[5]

Essentially this reiterates the dictum quoted above: the image of one's suffering, the formulation of one's future, however "true," is "what one is not" and hence a lie. The gulf between feeling and the articulation of feeling is unbridgeable. On the other hand, this same inner reality to which one's own mind is powerless to give shape, instantly identifies itself with the formulation of others' experience; just because the linear dimension of time has been captured once and for all, however inadequately, in a written document, the human mind eagerly holds up the chance formulations of, say, a letter as the clarifying mirror-image of its own enigma:

> If our letters cannot match our own feelings—naturally, there are varying degrees of this, passing imperceptibly into one another in both directions—if even at our best, expressions like

"indescribable," "inexpressible," or "so sad," or "so beautiful," followed by a rapidly collapsing "that"-clause, must perpetually come to our assistance, then as if in compensation we have been given the ability to comprehend what another person has written with at least the same degree of calm exactitude which we lack when we confront our own letter-writing. Our ignorance of those feelings which alternately make us crumple up and pull open again the letter in front of us, this very ignorance becomes knowledge the moment we are compelled to limit ourselves to this letter, to believe only what it says, and thus to find it perfectly expressed and perfect in expression, as is only right, if we are to see a clear road into what is most human. (9 December 1911)[6]

When juxtaposed, these diary entries, written less than a month apart, suggest very strongly the synthesis of perception which will enable Kafka to achieve his "breakthrough." If, without losing the skepticism that prevents him from identifying his own life with its metaphysical "model," he can manage to stand outside that life and view it as if it were being recorded by a stranger, then bleakly confusing subjectivity will acquire the patina of the time, both personal and historical, that is being lived.

The paradox here is the notion of "standing outside" oneself, but Kafka devoted much of his incidental writing to the elaboration of such paradoxes. The "development" manifest in Kafka's work results from a fundamental absence of "inward" development. Ceaselessly Kafka elaborates metaphorically his unchanging predicament; and as most apparent self-contradictions turn out to be refinements of his paradoxical thinking, it seems legitimate to me to use later material to shed light on the crucial months of gestation from the autumn of 1911 to 22 September 1912. Thus what Kafka did *not* mean by "standing outside" himself is graphically stated in a diary entry on 9 December 1913:

> Hatred of active introspection. Explanations of one's soul, such as: Yesterday I was so, and for this reason; today I am so, and for this reason. It is not true, not for this reason and not for that reason, and therefore also not so and so. To put up with oneself calmly, without being precipitate, to live as one must, not to chase one's tail like a dog.[7]

This kind of "self-observation" is simply an abandonment of the skepticism which, in 1911, prevented Kafka from "explaining" his own life in terms of the life model of the bachelor. As his life continued and seemed to fulfill his gloomy early prophecies in every detail, the temptation to "explain himself away" could only be combated by his growing self-awareness as an artist. For the ideal alternative in the diary entry—"put up with oneself calmly"—was of course not available to Kafka, whose self-hatred, while not my concern here, was undeniable. Self-observation without self-analysis was the only course open to him if the needed fictional shape were to be gleaned from his life in its historical context:

> This inescapable duty to observe oneself: if someone else is observing me, naturally I have to observe myself too; if none observes me, I have to observe myself all the closer. (7 November 1921)[8]

The ability to "mythologize" himself was matched in his years of maturity by the ability to "demythologize" history; as he could stand outside the shape of his own life, so he could enter into and skeptically dismantle the stories of the past (in December 1911 even a letter seemed invulnerable). The most striking example is Kafka's version of Alexander the Great, who decided to opt for a quiet life, to withdraw from the light of history before he had entered it, "because of the mere weight of his own body."[9]

The weakness of "The Urban World," then, does not lie in its detachment from the central figure, but in its removal of the observation point to a position *outside* Oskar's consciousness (Kafka is not wholly consistent about this—and why should he be in a sketch?—"entering" Oskar momentarily with the phrase, "became aware only when he spoke how he had been running"). If the hero is not the observer of his own actions (and if Kafka makes no attempt to establish an independent narrator, something he was not to do until the "reports" of his later years), two difficulties arise. First, as has been discussed above, the discontinuity of the characters' reactions becomes enigmatic, the vehemence of their emotions merely puzzling. The second problem is really the same one stated differently: the human protagonists, lacking any mediating consciousness, come unnaturally close to the reader, keying their rhetoric up to the roles they are playing. The son is conscious only of being a son, the father of being a father; this falsifies the essential indirectness with which the human mind perceives these matters. The emergence of the archetypal confrontation into the open in "The Judgment" is overwhelming precisely because of the lifelong repression of the truth evoked by the story. Indirectness, involuntary revelation, is the key to Kafka's mature style, not because he wants to complicate the truth, but because existence as Kafka experienced it seemed to require the repression, not only of all direct perceptions of truth, but also of the self-interest that shapes what actually is experienced:

> It is an old habit of mine, at the point when an impression has reached its greatest degree of purity, whether of joy or pain, not to allow it to run its salutary course through all my being, but rather to cloud and dispel its purity by new, unexpected, weak impressions. It is not that I evilly intend my own harm, I am only too weak to bear the purity of that impression. Instead of admitting this weakness, which alone would be right, because in revealing itself it calls forth other forces to its support, I rather quietly and with seeming arbitrariness try to evoke new impressions in an effort to help myself. (30 October 1911)[10]

As the momentum of these sentences grows, what begins as an attempt at description turns into an evocation of an inner drama in which the negative term "weakness" (*Schwäche*) acquires an independent dynamism that effectively supersedes its original connotations. A fictional form that could embody this microscopic world of perception, repression, and ceaseless analysis had not yet been devised. Kafka's dismantling of conventions extends to language itself. Words and thoughts seek meaning in terms of each other: there is no perspective, no stable center to the relationship, only endless stratagems by which the mind tries both to absorb and to resist its perceptions, building defenses, evading commitments, sealing off pain. For this endeavor both descriptive fiction ("what one is not") and the solipsistic monodrama developed by Schnitzler are inadequate. As the odd perspectives of "The Urban World" suggest, Kafka is searching for a narrative convention that will allow both the vulnerability and the fundamental dishonesty of the human mind to achieve expression.

During the six-month period of 11 October to March 1912, a period unusually well annotated in his diaries, Kafka was involved with both the work and the people of the Jewish theater in Prague, in ways that seem to have brought him closer to "happiness" than any other experience recorded by him. I do not intend to argue that this involvement with the theater influenced his work in tangible details:[11] theater and fiction remain separate literary modes. What Kafka learned from the theater, first of all, was that conveying "reality" involves many conventions, that communication is impossible without them. In portraying a character on stage, the skillful actor exercises a compulsion on the audience comparable to the effect on the reader of another's memoirs or letters; he imposes an order on the character's various facets so that they seem "inevitable," and this he can only achieve by *not* identifying with the character, for such total involvement would result in disorder, disarray—and the audience's disbelief. In a long meditation[12] on the mediating role of the actor Kafka analyzes what he feels to be his own lack of mimetic discipline in terms that transcend technical questions:

> My urge to imitate has nothing of the actor in it, its chief lack is unity .... I have a decided urge to imitate them in their details, the way certain people manipulate walking sticks, the way they hold their hands, the movements of their fingers, and I can do it without any effort. But this very effortlessness, this thirst for imitation, sets me apart from the actor, because this effortlessness reflects itself in the fact that no one is aware that I am imitating .... Far beyond this external imitation, however, goes the inner, which is often so striking and strong that there is no room at all within me to observe and verify it, and it first confronts me in my memory. But here the imitation is so complete and replaces my own self with so immediate a suddenness that, even assuming it could be made visible at all, it would be unbearable on the stage. The spectator cannot be asked to endure what passes beyond the bounds of play-acting. If an actor who is supposed to thrash another according to the plot really does thrash him, out of excitement, out of an excess of emotion, and the other actor screams in pain, then the spectator must become a man and intervene. (30 December 1911)[13]

The crucial difference between himself and the actor, Kafka feels, is the actor's "position on the inside (Platz im Innern)," the separate individuality which "observes" his role in the act of giving it physical presence. What distinguishes Kafka's viewpoint from any tendency towards Brechtian "alienation" is that Kafka regards the actor's separateness as the indispensable element in creating the audience's "involvement." The actor relates his role to the other actors, to the scenery, to the audience, to the historical time of the performance, and by preempting all these possible escape routes in the audience's mind he prevents them from becoming "men" and breaking the bond of necessity between them and the stage action. The actor, in other words, includes the audience's potential skepticism in his presentation. The script of the play is a kind of mythical core, an unnatural concentration of human emotion which is essentially "other" than the world of the audience. As Kafka notes, it is the actor's task to join the world of the audience and the myth of the play in a seamless closed circuit; the actor "presents" the play in such a way that the audience does not notice the "improbable" elements which ensure the forward movement it has come to regard as "natural":

> Granted that the audience does not see everything from the point of view of the author, that even he is surprised by the performance, it is still the author who had the play with all its details within himself, who moved along from detail to detail, and who only because he assembled all the details in the speeches has given them dramatic weight and force. Because of this the drama in its highest development achieves an unbearable humanization which it is the task of the actor—with his role blowing loosely and in tatters about him—to draw down, to make bearable. The drama therefore hovers in the air, but not like a roof carried along on a storm, rather like a whole building whose foundation walls have been torn up out of the earth with a force which today is still close to madness. (29 October 1911)[14]

This last image powerfully suggests the relationship Kafka sought to establish between his own stories and external reality. Through language and its concomitant, human reason, the stories are rooted in the tangible, familiar world; but this world has suddenly become a stage; its "foundation walls" have been ripped out and an action of mythological proportions is forcing its way into existence. The protagonist of the story has the task of reconciling the old world with the new, but what brings his situation much closer to "madness" than the actor's is that their positions are reversed. The actor's "self" is detached from his role, modulating his involvement to produce a mimetic effect; but the Kafka hero's "self" is totally absorbed by the unfolding events—it is "torn up out of the earth" of predictability, lacking any vantage point outside the role it is called on to play. The Kafka hero is not so much deprived of his freedom as required to define it—a paradoxical formulation which suggests the limits within which the play of the self is acted out. These limits are of course arbitrary—and arbitrariness conditions Kafka's world, generating a feeling in the reader (and occasionally in the hero) that the "real play" is taking place elsewhere, that almost all the hero-actor's decisions are irrelevant. One of them is probably crucial, but to the hero it may well not appear as a decision at all; the moment in which he finally loses control will pass unnoticed:

> Sometimes it seems that the play is resting up in the flies, the actors have drawn down strips of it the ends of which they hold in their hands or have wound about their bodies for the play, and that only now and then a strip that is difficult to release carries an actor, to the terror of the audience, up in the air. (29 October 1911)[15]

Awareness of the theatrical analogy underlying Kafka's world helps to overcome two common misinterpretations of the hero's responses to his situation. There is first the old notion that Kafka's characters are trapped by "fate" and grapple with a force outside themselves. As we shall see, the Kafka hero himself does not think this: Walter Sokel has ably demonstrated how the hero at once recognizes the "drama" as emerging from a part of himself he has repressed, challenging him to become whole again. While the hero is not able to respond directly to the challenge, he is deeply curious and is drawn towards events, at the same time consciously denying their significance. The Kafka hero's entry onto the stage of the self offers at least the possibility of meaning where none had existed. The opposite error is to regard the perpetual disengagement of the hero's consciousness as escapism, moral weakness. If only he would show more generosity, more love, this argument goes, he would be able to grasp the opportunities offered him. But Kafka is not interested in condemning his characters: they condemn themselves and need no judge but themselves. The purpose of the narrative theater, as I have tried to show, is to present a kind of foreshortened life story from the point of view of the character living it, which at the same time has the "inevitability" of a story seen from the outside.

The stories are in one sense deterministic: the drama emerges from the character of the hero and moves inexorably to its end. But on another level each moment is absolute: the same detached consciousness that prevents the hero from merging fully with his hole is also distilling more and more of the truth from the situation, so that, with almost mathematical logic, the hero achieves some clarity about himself just as events are moving too fast for his understanding to be of any use. As the central character functions on two levels, so does the reader's reaction to the story; while he watches the simultaneous construction and destruction of a life defined by failure, and learns to see a self-defeating rhythm in the hero's reactions, the reader is never free of the thought that a particular situation, if only through lucky chance, will produce the "right" reaction in the hero. The tension of a Kafka story is rooted in the persistence of this possibility and in the suggestion that only one right move is necessary. What this positive result might be can only be hinted at, but it is a "nothing" that could at any point become "something" and thrust the whole determinist shape of the story into the realm of illusion: "The number of hiding places is infinite and there is only one escape, but there are as many possibilities of escape as there are hiding places."[16] At the outset the hero asserts that the drama engulfing him is illusory; and even as the drama establishes itself as the indisputable reality, the possibility is never absent that it too, like the roots of the "tree trunks in the snow," is ultimately insubstantial.

The ease with which the theatrical mode can thus be restated in the perceptual terminology of Kafka's early years illustrates its value to him. The method of antithesis always tends to disintegrate its subject, systematically undermining any "solid ground" that seems to have been achieved. The theatrical analogy, by contrast, is essentially "constructive," fertile with illusions. A framework is set around the story, a theater complete with artificial scenery; within this framework one fictional assertion is as valid as any other. The immediacy of the dramatic situation is not to be doubted; the hero appears, to the reader and sometimes to himself, to be making vital decisions concerning his very existence. But we can never be sure these decisions are so important. They remain within the confines of the theater, and the "real world" behind the scenery keeps its enigmatic distance. Speculation about it among the characters on stage takes two superficially opposed directions: "reality" is the uneventful world of day-to-day business—or it is "salvation," "acquittal," or some other term for the advent of the telos. Gradually, however, these two avenues of speculation describe a circle and merge, dissolving in the penumbra of legend: the attention of all participants is redirected to the stage, than which nothing more "real" can be conceived after all. Even when the hero dies, the scenery remains in place. The very scope for self-expression afforded him by the theater is ultimately limiting: the "meaning" of his role, if any, is to be found in the accumulation of individual scenes. Pressing towards a "final act" that never materializes, the hero is repeatedly thrust back to his starting point.

4 "The Judgment"

That Georg Bendemann is a character divided against himself is obvious enough: the problem for the critic is to locate the source of this division. In postulating a source at the "deepest" level possible, Walter Sokel dissolves the "figure" of Georg as he presents himself to the reader into a hierarchy of compartmentalized urges. The results are contradictory; while the observing, rational self is a "façade" and the instinctual substratum expresses the "true self" repressed by the façade, it also appears that the true self is "regressive" and the façade embodies the "responsible human being." The only way out of this maze of conflicting value judgments is to assert that oneness is superior to duality. This Sokel does in finding the conclusion of "The Judgment," with its total negation of Georg's individuality, to be a "resurrection."[1] As Lawrence Ryan points out, his view runs counter to the whole atmosphere of the story and rests heavily on an a-priori definition of the river's symbolic function:

> It is by no means the case that Kafka affirms the guilt-ridden submergence in the "stream of life" and, as it were, glorifies the extinction of the individual life in those blood-ties which hold together the family in the most primitive sense. Rather, precisely the opposite occurs in this work, namely Kafka's liberation into an artist's state, to which he remains loyal throughout his life.[2]

Ryan's view is that the ascetic friend in Russia has found the correct way of life. In a modernized form, Sokel and Ryan represent the two traditional approaches to Kafka's characters. For Sokel, the archetypal forces at work in the story are so strong that it hardly makes sense to talk of Georg as an individual; the reader is merely witnessing a fate so inevitable that it can scarcely be termed tragic, the dissolution of a life that has never functionally existed. Ryan, on the other hand, sees Georg as all too much the individual, a man who could have chosen otherwise, whose way of life is presented to the reader for implicit condemnation.

The figure of Georg Bendemann encompasses both of these readings without being limited by them: he is closer to "everyman" than Ryan allows, yet more firmly delineated as an individual than Sokel's approach suggests. Kafka has certainly utilized the archetypal conflict between father and son as the motor force of his story. But his focus is on the mechanism of Georg's responses, the sequence of actions and through processes that the reader transmutes into a human identity. The first part of the story shows that Georg is a man who, to an exceptional extent, stands outside his own life, ceaselessly arranging and defining it in terms of the commonsense norms embedded in language. He has so ordered his role by means of "rational" categories of behavior that he can no longer perceive the instinctual, self-serving purposes that have produced those categories. "The Judgment" is a precarious, unrepeatable structure combining an undisguised portrayal of life's most basic power conflict with a protagonist so self-absorbed that he has come to deny the existence of any conflict whatever. In order to synthesize these extremes Kafka has combined ordered thinking with its antithesis in such a manner that the reader can no longer distinguish one from the other. On initial reading the first half of the story seems sane, real, and undramatic, while the second half is a dramatic concentration of two whole lives, surreal to the point of insanity. Subsequent readings, while not invalidating this impression, set another one beside it: at the outset Georg is consciously transforming all "reality" into a mental drama centered on himself, while at the end the destruction of these mental categories forces Georg to a self-annihilation void of dramatic purpose, a helpless acknowledgment that his entire consciousness is now, quite literally, lifeless.

Georg interprets a dynamic, fluid situation in static terms; the life he sees is like a chessboard, on which every shift is reasoned out and takes place according to rules of his own making. But as he does not acknowledge his own motivation towards accretion of power, so he is always taken by surprise by the independent action of others, for example the friend's interest in the indifferent matters of which Georg had been writing. On Georg's mental chessboard the friend has been pushed ever farther away as he represents a life of integrity on which Georg has turned his back; into his orbit he is now drawing his "queen," the "girl from a well-to-do family (Mädchen aus wohlhabender Familie)" —and as for the father, Kafka himself sums it up: "he believes he has his father within him (er glaubt den Vater in sich zu haben)."[3]

The intensely visual quality of Georg's thoughts is emphasized in Kafka's commentary. The dangerous move Georg is contemplating is the recall of the friend into the group close to him on the chessboard. If he could have the friend "within him" as well as his father, then the shape of his life would be complete, containing both the authenticity of the past and the moral validity given by the friend's integrity. The danger lies in the autonomous, as it were, magnetic, force possessed by the friend. By bringing the one unabsorbed element back into the almost closed circle of his life, Georg opens the way for the father to escape, turn over the chessboard, and, instead of scattering the pieces, absorb them into himself. Kafka says of the fiancée that she lives in the story "only in relation to the friend (nur durch die Beziehung zum Freund)"; in a deeper sense, this is also true of the father. He gains his power from "the common bond" (*die Gemeinsamkeit*), from the fact that Georg has chosen to open up what had seemed to be closed; as Kafka puts it, Georg "rummages voluptuously in this consciousness of what they have in common (wühlt in diesem Gemeinsamen mit Wollust)." The ultimate "voluptuousness" lies for Georg in the entry into his father's room to display the letter, the seal of his final triumph, as if to say, "Soon you will be joined in this prison by the person through whose integrity alone, because the memory of it persists in me, you have any remaining hold over my life." The result of this premature celebration of power is conveyed visually by Kafka as, drawn out by the friend's magnetism, "the father rises up out of what they have in common, out of the friend (aus dem Gemeinsamen, dem Freund, der Vater hervorsteigt)." Then, in the most striking image of all, "what they had in common is now all piled up around the father (Das Gemeinsame ist alles um den Vater aufgetürmt)": the constructed world of Georg's mind, in which every element has its own compartment, has suddenly been replaced by the unmediated world of direct confrontation. Georg's elaborate tactics, however, are geared exclusively to the indirect conflict of his mental theater, and are ineffective on any other stage. The father is not really powerful; his strength is only "enough for you (genug für dich)," in effect handed to him by Georg's false move in connection with the friend.

It is wrong to lend undue weight to the archetypal nature of the father-son conflict; as with Gregor's parasitism, this is to attach oneself to the obvious elements of the story and neglect the specific role of the hero in bringing about his own end. Georg's defeat has nothing to do with fate or retribution; true, he has behaved without any regard for morality, but moral issues do not decide questions of power. What happens is that Georg, as he savors the coming triumph, neglects the formality, the indirectness, that underlies his image of order, entering almost sensually into his own world of "play." The word "playful" (*spielerisch*),[4] which in the first paragraph alerts the reader to the significance of Georg's letter, can be understood on several levels. Georg is being consciously "casual," concealing from himself, as he usually does, the import of his own action; he is making a gambler's "play," staking his past winnings to achieve what he thinks is a virtually certain final victory; and he is staging an internal drama in which all the pieces move according to his own predetermined vision.

Sokel points to the "dramatic" sequence of imagery in "The Judgment": "When, at the beginning of the story, he had looked out upon the bridge, a quiet emptiness, a kind of frozen suspension of life, prevailed. His dying re-animates life."[5] But whereas he regards the story as a "dionysiac" tragedy, even inflating the laconic final sentence into a "resurrection," I see it rather as an inversion of the Promethean story, an attempt at displacing established order not through "excess" of life but through its degradation by means of psychic ingestion. The letter to the friend is the act of hubris, the assertion that Georg can incorporate into his wholly egocentric existence the element most alien to it: human integrity. What the reader witnesses in the first part of the story, in the guise of rational thought processes, is the mental drama leading up to the act of hubris. A vital point is that these rationalizations are not "thoughts" in the sense that Georg is experiencing the actual process of self-deception and imparting it to the reader directly. On the contrary, Georg has *already* sealed the letter whose contents are the outcome of this sequence of reasoning. Georg is reenacting, in the long-established terminology of his own script, the sequence of events which has culminated in this final gamble.

The story's second paragraph, which presents facts only slightly colored by Georg's viewpoint, can be legitimately read as Georg's "thoughts," moving from the just-completed letter to the ascetic enigma who is its object. But the third paragraph reveals immediately the level to which Georg has moved. "What could one write to such a man, who had obviously run off the rails ... (Was sollte man einem solchen Manne schreiben, der sich offenbar verrannt hatte ...)": these words show in three respects how Georg has shifted from the actual friend to the reconstruction of the friend necessary to his own subjective drama. First, the rhetorical question itself, given that the letter is already

sealed, shows Georg moving from the present moment to the reconstruction of events that have led up to this moment; second, the gen-
eralizing phrase "such a man" is an attempt to deny the friend's
uncomfortable uniqueness, to dismantle him, as it were, into components that Georg can assimilate into his own world view; and finally,
the imagery of "who had obviously run off the rails" just does not follow from the decisive words, "adjusted himself to being permanently
a bachelor (richtete sich so für ein endgültiges Junggesellentum ein),"[6]
which conclude the preceding paragraph. The friend has been allowed
to describe himself just enough for the reader to be aware that Georg
is here presenting an outsider's caricature, a caricature essential to the
picture of his own sympathetic superiority which he then develops. The
friend is not the vacillating failure Georg would have him appear to be,
and as Georg's reasoning moves ever further from the minimal facts
of the second paragraph, it becomes clear that the friend is simply "the
other," both a persisting obligation from Georg's earlier way of life and
a symbol of moral independence that Georg cannot reconcile with his
own unacknowledged surrender to a wholly selfish mode of living.

What is troubling Georg and causing him to review once more all
the moves he has made thus far is that the writing of the letter goes
against all that the ruthless caution of his instincts had told him. Originally he had decided, quite rightly from his point of view, not to invite
the friend to his wedding. After marriage, Georg's way of life would
be finally legitimized, because his ambitions would be officially justified
by the firm grounding and perpetuation of the family (as Kafka points
out in his commentary, the reason the fiancée is "easily driven away"
is that she is not yet part of Georg's "circle of blood relationship"). As
a married man Georg would be in a stronger position to build protective rationalizations against the friend's integrity. Until then he is in the
typically exposed position of the Kafka hero, suspended between two
worlds. A bachelor, he has turned his back on the insights of bache-
lordom, with their concomitant insecurities; but the persisting need to
justify to himself his behavior toward the friend shows that he has not
finally entered the "swamp world" (*Schlammwelt*)[7] of unreflecting
egocentricity. And so Georg has been pushing the friend ever further
from him, weaving explanations for the friend's behavior that are ex-
quisitely compounded of fiction and cliché. "Two years ago [Georg's]
mother had died . . . his friend had of course been informed of that and
had expressed his sympathy in a letter phrased so dryly that the grief
caused by such an event, one had to conclude, could not be realized in
a distant country."[8] The simple explanation for the friend's "dryness,"
of course, is that he is annoyed at not hearing the news directly from

Georg; Georg conceals this from himself first with the ambivalent *wohl*,[9] a word used with increasing frequency as the rationale for his own behavior becomes shakier, then with the resounding cliché about "grief," a phrase all the more grotesque because of Georg's own calculating, unemotional tone.

This process culminates in Georg's "putting the friend to bed" with his letters on indifferent matters. "All he desired was to leave undisturbed the idea of the home town which his friend must have built up to his own content during the long interval."[10] Once again the indicative mood is modified by *wohl* (contained here in "must have"), but this time Georg presumes to penetrate the friend's actual state of mind with his speculations, having previously confined himself to reorganizing the facts. He cannot of course know that the friend prefers a nostalgic image of his home town; nevertheless, this is presented in the indicative, his reconstruction of the friend having finally supplanted the original in Georg's inner drama.

The essential turning point of the story, as the language indicates, is not Georg's entry into his father's room but the scene with the fiancée. To take an analogy from a "real" play, this resembles Macbeth's scene with Lady Macbeth before the murder of Duncan. Like Lady Macbeth, the fiancée encourages Georg to adopt a course so rash, yet so inviting in its possibilities, that he had not dared to admit it to himself. Like Macbeth, however, Georg had betrayed his obsession by talking about it with noticeable frequency to the person he regards as his firm ally. The movement of this paragraph throws new light on the oddly tense language of the previous paragraph describing Georg's last dealings with the friend: "And so it happened to Georg that three times in three fairly widely separated letters he had told his friend about the engagement of an unimportant man to an equally unimportant girl . . . ."[11] Nothing merely "happens" to people in fiction, least of all in Kafka's fiction; when writing to the friend, Georg cannot stop referring to the term "engagement," just as, when talking to the fiancée, he cannot stop talking about the friend. Georg presents to his fiancée the reconstructed image of his relationship with the friend with such obsessive frequency that she comes to accept his version of matters as "true": not only is the friend in a very bad way, but Georg cares for him exceedingly and thinks only of how to alleviate his condition. Thus does Georg's imagined order of things tip over into reality, and the unacknowledged, insanely bold ambition of winning friend and fiancée simultaneously is forced out into the open by the fiancée's innocent remark: "If you have such friends, Georg, you shouldn't ever have got engaged at all."[12] All she means is that the friend seems to occupy

Georg's thoughts more than she does. But Georg's reply thrusts the matter immediately into the atmosphere of *Macbeth:* "Well, we're both to blame for that (Ja, das ist unser beider Schuld)." His constant mention of the friend has had all along the unacknowledged purpose of provoking her into just such a remark; now that she has made it she moves, in his mind, into the position of close ally (or, as the word "blame" implies, accomplice). At last he feels the strength to move from barely acknowledged imaginings to a real act of hubris; this will be the easier, so he thinks, as the movement into reality (the friend's mind) will be a gradual one, mediated by a letter over which he retains complete control. The sheer impudence of Georg's final cliché to rationalize his change of direction reminds the reader how completely mental constructs have replaced any kind of self-awareness: "That's the kind of man I am and he'll just have to take me as I am (So bin ich und so hat er mich hinzunehmen . . .)."

The scene in the father's room can be divided into two sections, the first ending with the father's leap from under the bedclothes. During this first part the reader sees the progressive hollowing out of Georg's consciousness and is prepared for the total dislocation of the final pages. The story is still very much a "game," but suddenly Georg is not in control of the game. We have seen that the basis of Georg's game with reality is physical and mental distance; as the father says, he locks himself in his office and there he spins the web of controlled relationships into which he has been trying to incorporate the friend. What the father does is trap Georg into sheer physical closeness to reality, so that, when he finally launches his attack, Georg will be unable to retreat (retreat was in fact available to Oskar, the hero of "The Urban World": under attack from the father he opened the door, albeit with difficulty, and left). The father's strategy is, by his pretended obtuseness over the friend, to give Georg the illusion that he can still win and so draw him irrevocably into the conflict. From the ordered theater of his subjectivity Georg is compelled to act on the father's stage of total unpredictability; accustomed to absorbing each successive event into his mental scheme of things, he reacts anxiously to each statement of the father's, desperately hoping to restore some kind of order. But with every remark the father opens up new areas Georg had thought sealed forever; because Georg's "assets" have been totally absorbed into his ordered world, with the destruction of that order they drain away from him instantly, leaving him with "nothing but his awareness of the father (nichts mehr als den Blick auf den Vater)."[13]

From the moment of entering the room, Georg is afflicted with involuntary thoughts—"My father is still a giant of a man (mein Vater ist noch immer ein Riese)"—that loosen his control over his own actions. Indeed the immediate physical impact of his father in his own dark room—whether or not we choose to gloss the point psychoanalytically—causes Georg to submit, as it were, to his father's movements: "vacantly" (*verloren*) is a doubly significant word when applied to so self-controlled a character as Georg. As Georg spells out for the third time (previously to himself and to his fiancée) his "reasons" for not telling the friend of his engagement, the reader feels the accumulated feebleness of the clichés; Georg is still following his own script, but even he seems to feel its hollowness, judging by his overelaborate responses to the father's abrupt questions.

The father then draws Georg more deeply into the conflict with his deliberately "moderate" rehearsal of Georg's faults, culminating in the "trivial affair" (*Kleinigkeit*): "Do you really have this friend in St. Petersburg? (Hast du wirklich diesen Freund in Petersburg?)." By this question the father encourages Georg to think that his mind is wandering and so draws Georg into solicitous physical contact; at the same time the question goes to the central weakness of Georg's position— Georg used to have a friend, he hopes to regain the friend on his own terms, but it is debatable whether at this moment he actually "has" a friend. Georg falls into the trap: from this point he seems less and less able to "think," being aware only of physical groupings. He loses his sense of proportion to the point where he seeks "victory" on a purely physical level, through putting the father to bed: "Meanwhile Georg had succeeded in lowering his father down again (Währenddessen war es Georg gelungen, den Vater wieder niederzusetzen . . .)." But the physical is the father's element; by choosing to fight on the father's terms, Georg dooms himself. The father's toying with Georg's watch chain has been interpreted variously, and I do not wish to argue with symbolisms that have meaning in the context of a different overall approach. In relation to Georg's life as he has organized it, his "dreadful feeling (schreckliches Gefühl)" is a response to the total intimacy of the gesture, the antithesis of the wholly controlled aloofness which is the foundation of Georg's adult life. We have seen Georg "putting to bed" the friend metaphorically, through patronizing letters; to attempt to do the same thing in actual physical terms is to forfeit the "distance" upon which Georg's power depends.

Upon the father's resurgence Georg, for so long a puppet-master, is now himself a puppet who can do no more than react to the father's thrusts, on both the physical and the verbal level: " 'But attend to me!' cried his father, and Georg, almost distracted, ran towards the bed to take everything in, yet came to a stop halfway."[14] There is no "logical" connection between the father's command and Georg's response. Georg's mind, accustomed to order, attaches itself to the disorder of the bed; he rushes to put things right, stops as if afflicted by the absurdity of taking refuge in a world of things so long despised. But now everything is concentrated into physical images. He who had systematically detached his friend from all recognizable individuality can now see only a physical image of the friend; despite everything, the friend is *standing*, an action symbolizing his survival—all Georg can do is to run convulsively. "A long time ago he had firmly made up his mind to watch closely every least movement (Vor einer langen Weile hatte er sich fest entschlossen, alles vollkommen genau zu beobachten . . . .)"; a symptom of Georg's total dislocation is that this resolve, so characteristic of what used to be his approach to all situations, comes into being merely as a memory of a past receding so rapidly that it already seems "a long time ago."

Georg's last independent act of self-expression is the utterance "You comedian! (Komödiant!)." Only on the most superficial level, as he at once realizes, is this a defiant remark; in all other respects it is a final surrender. Georg, by definition an "actor" playing his own life according to a script, hands this last attribute to his father. If the father, and not he himself, is the actor, then he has no refuge left; the only hope of recovery lay in Georg's withdrawing from the scene, whether physically like the hero of "The Urban World," or mentally by somehow absorbing the father's attack in his own game plan. Now he has not only played the father's game and lost, he has explicitly acknowledged his father's superiority. All Georg's remaining thoughts, words, and reactions express this final crumbling of his mental theater. With the vain hope that the father will fall and the mental incantation about the father's pockets we are in the realm of primitive magic; as the immediacy of the objects under the father's control overwhelms him, Georg lunges for some ritual potency in them that might yet save him. The helpless line "Georg made a grimace of disbelief (Georg machte Grimassen, als glaube er das nicht)" and the exclamation "ten thousand times! (Zehntausendmal!)" reduce the magic to a still more rudimentary level; long unaware of the substance of the father's speeches, Georg responds like a circus clown, hoping that a mere negative grimace or its counterpart, a feeble exaggeration, will somehow divert his father from the assault. The theatrical theme comes into the open once again, with Georg's last response: "So you've been lying in wait for me! (Du hast mir also aufgelauert!)" As the father pitilessly points out, this sentence is a cliché that would have fitted into the script earlier. It has no relevance to what the father has just said; it is a phrase plucked by Georg from some melodrama in what remains of his memory, uttered as if to show merely that he is not yet dead. At most it is, like the earlier "You comedian!" a confirmation that the father has defeated him at his own game.

Sokel regards Georg's last words, "Dear parents, I have always loved you, all the same (Liebe Eltern, ich habe euch doch immer geliebt)," as expressing a genuine reemergence of the "innocent child (unschuldiges Kind)" from under the layers of the "devilish human being (teuflischer Mensch)." To me, Georg is an actor to the last. His death signifies no more than the final negation of his existence, an unravelling of time back through childhood to a starting point before the onset of consciousness. The rhythm which is to be codified into the ritual structure of *The Trial* is here presented with radical starkness: if consciousness implies manipulation, then the collapse of the mental theater involves the extinction of every trace of consciousness. Georg's last words are merely a corollary of his acceptance of the father's death sentence; having lost the struggle, he adopts the victor's point of view wholeheartedly, that is, his personality is simply eliminated by the father's will, so that at the end he says what the father wants him to say. There is no reconciliation here, just final defeat. In death Georg plays the role at the farthest remove from the role he had adopted in life, that of dutiful son. Georg has denied himself (as he denied his friend) to such an extent that his death does more than negate his life, it replaces it with an image—"innocent child"—of his father's choosing.

5   "The Metamorphosis"

A common error in Kafka criticism is to align individual works under a single rubric. Because "The Judgment" relates the destruction of a falsely based individuality, Gregor Samsa is forced into the same mold, with guilt and parasitism read between the lines of the text; because "The Judgment" shows the resurgence of a father, crucial importance is attached to the uniform and bearing of Herr Samsa. But Gregor has little in common with Georg Bendemann. For one thing, his life is not notably successful. For another, if he has "exploited" his family, Kafka would surely have indicated the fact more clearly; the father's depressed state is simply explicable in terms of the collapse of his business five years earlier. And the person who affects Gregor's outlook decisively in the course of the story is not his father but his sister Grete. True, Kafka wanted to publish "The Stoker," "The Judgment," and "The Metamorphosis" under the collective title "Sons (Die Söhne)"; but the plural noun is just as suggestive of essential differences as it is of a common pattern. "The Stoker" presents Rossmann's emergence from anonymity, with no preordained tendencies except a recreative commitment to an ordered world. "The Judgment" shows the dramatic and instantaneous collapse of a man who has carried the idea of order to the point of aspiring to replace reality itself by his elaborately staged mental categories. "The Metamorphosis" begins, in a sense, where "The Judgment" leaves off. Georg Bendemann has so alienated himself from the process of living that the functional bond between self and world is severed; his individuality is, literally and figuratively, submerged in the organic substance of life. Gregor too has become alienated, but not, like Georg, through an active combination of will and imaginative distance. Rather, Gregor is deficient in both qualities; his life resembles that of an automaton, and the organic world invades him in the form of the transformation, not to kill him, but to compel him to live. In the compulsion laid upon Gregor to develop a new identity, Kafka has in one sense returned to the zero point of "The Stoker." But while Gregor, like Karl Rossmann, is effectively cut off from his own past, he is, unlike Karl, surrounded by that past both physically and mentally. His new life, by definition lacking a future, impels him to a reanimation of his past that effectively amounts to living that past for the first time.

The theatrical analogy, which has been shown to be essential to the structure of "The Judgment," is here so obvious as to be for the most part unnoticeable. The split between human mind and insect body compels Gregor to look at his existence from the outside, to formulate a role, a pattern of living, for himself. Gregor's conscientious, if objectively hopeless, struggle for an identity is what gives the story its human breadth; if "The Metamorphosis" is nothing more than a "punitive fantasy,"[1] then Kafka's only purpose is to portray Gregor's obtuse slowness in recognizing the need for his own death. As Lawrence Ryan says:

> According to Sokel, Gregor becomes a "true son" through this affirmation of his own death, indeed it is only by doing so that he realizes his "own being." But it seems to us to border on inhumanity if one claims to hear in this something like the voice of life itself, affirming the instinctual, biologically conditioned sequence of generations as opposed to all emancipation of the individual. Kafka is not recognizable in such an interpretation.[2]

The development of Gregor's quest for an identity can be divided into six stages, each section of the story containing a kind of caesura, a point at which the nature of Gregor's responses noticeably changes. Each change is correlated with a shift in Gregor's relationship to his sister. Her role is structurally analogous to that of the friend in "The Judgment." We have seen how, as Kafka's commentary emphasizes, the friend is the axis on which Georg's relationship to his father revolves: without the friend, the father would have no power over Georg. So it is here: although the father causes Gregor's death physically, it is the sister who opens the way to this development and to Gregor's acceptance of it. Gregor is never under any illusions about his father's attitude, taking it fully into account in his attempts to form an identity; about the sister he achieves clarity only gradually. His relationship with her is both analogous and antithetical to that of Georg Bendemann with the friend in Russia: Georg exploits his friend, Gregor is exploited by his sister. We are told that she has always been "close" to him, a phrase expressive of her mirroring function. Although Kafka goes far in suggesting independent motivation in the sister, the result is always to counterpoint and broaden the scope of Gregor's inner drama, which is increasingly focused on her; of prime importance is the fact that Grete represents the "world," the exclusively human realm as symbolized in its positive form by her violin playing. Her negative function lies in her unyielding hostility to Gregor's efforts at achieving a median identity between the human and the animal. This is not to say that she "destroys" Gregor any more than the friend (or indeed the father) destroys Georg Bendemann; Georg destroys himself, and Gregor's death is inevitable from the moment of the transformation, inherent in the impossibility of "human beings living with such a creature (ein Zusammenleben von Menschen mit einem solchen Tier)" (Grete's words). The role of both Grete and the friend is that of catalyst, bringing into the open, for the hero himself as well as for the reader, the movement of the hero's consciousness.

It is only partially true that, as is often asserted, Gregor refuses to accept his transformation in the first part, talking about the office as if nothing had happened. Upon first awakening he responds quite directly to his condition—"It was no dream (Es war kein Traum)"— and when he first starts thinking of his job ("Oh God, he thought, what an exhausting job I've picked on!"),[3] there are extremely easy transitions between his thoughts and his exploration of his body, as the sentences about his "itching place (juckende Stelle)" make plain. The negative thoughts about his work are, as it were, induced by the transformation and harmonize with it. There is, I think, critical unanimity that Gregor has in some sense "willed" the transformation as a release from the inhuman monotony of his nominally human life; the animalistic suggestiveness of the fur-covered lady in his picture confirms this initial hypothesis. What deserves greater attention is the significance of the picture frame; we are told shortly by Gregor's mother that he had made it himself, indeed that carpentry, that basic manifestation of *homo faber*, is Gregor's only activity as an individual. If the picture in its frame is as important as its position in the story suggests (both here and in the furniture-removal scene), it indicates that, by slipping into the organic world, Gregor is also gaining a chance to reassert his individuality. The transformation leads inexorably towards death, to be sure, but it also gives Gregor the opportunity, not available to untransformed humanity, of building, within strictly circumscribed limits, a fresh identity from a zero point. Just because the scope of his activity is so limited, it is knowable in every detail and translatable into an "ordered" way of living; the self-dramatizing talent that destroys Georg Bendemann enables Gregor to continue living, as he absorbs every statement and gesture of his family into a new self-image.

But this is to look ahead. Part One of the story details the simultaneous movement of Gregor outwards, towards the "world," and inwards, to his new nature. This process has a rise and a fall, with a climax at the point where his culminating effort on behalf of his old identity (unlocking the door) coincides with a sudden calm awareness of the irrevocable change. Three tangible pressures push him away from his initial state of inquisitive self-absorption: the sight of the clock, the anxiety of his family, and finally the job itself in the person of the chief clerk. The geographical position of Gregor's room already suggests the dominating hold his family has over him; but in the sister's exhortation to open his door there is a hint that her demands on him are more total, less concerned for his residual humanity, than the others'. Gregor's response conveys a surprising brusqueness that already implies an ambivalence in his professed regard for her:

> However, Gregor had no intention of opening the door, but felt thankful for the prudent habit he had acquired in traveling of locking all doors during the night, even at home.[4]

The sister's influence on Gregor is strong; here, as elsewhere, the effect of her intervention is to take a decision for him that he does not really want to take. The sentence quoted suggests an almost petulant rejection; nevertheless, Gregor now decides to get up. Two words, in a repeated counterpoint, evoke the conflicting impulses in Gregor during the remainder of this section: "quiet" (*ruhig*) and "sensible" (*vernünftig*). Clichés of virtuous conduct derived from his old identity, these words take on new dimensions as they seem to point him in opposite directions. As he decides to get up they still operate in unison in his own mind—but only because his plan, a hasty response to his sister's insistent "normality," is a ludicrous fantasy:

> His immediate intention was to get up quietly without being disturbed, to put on his clothes and above all eat his breakfast, and only then to consider what else was to be done, since in bed, he was well aware, his meditations would come to no sensible conclusion.[5]

Gregor has in effect opted for reason rather than tranquillity, as the uncontrolled response of his "little legs" (*Beinchen*) indicates; as he tries to compel his body to conform to the dictates of his old identity, he fills his mind with the appropriate cliché: "But what's the use of lying idle in bed (Nur sich nicht im Bett unnütz aufhalten)." When the first attempt fails and it begins to dawn on Gregor that "peace" (*Ruhe*) is attainable only through self-adaptation to his new body, Gregor desperately reiterates the precepts of his old identity, especially the twin key words, as if to compel order by unleashing the full force of the moralizing rhetoric that has ruled his life hitherto:

> But when after a repetition of the same efforts he lay in his former position again, sighing, and watched his little legs struggling against each other more wildly than ever, if that were possible, and saw no way of bringing any order into this arbitrary confusion, he told himself again that it was impossible to stay in bed and that the most sensible course was to risk everything for the smallest hope of getting away from it. At the same time he did not forget meanwhile to remind himself that cool reflection, the coolest possible, was much better than desperate resolves.[6]

With the withdrawal of the props of his old life, symbolized by the blotting-out of the window by fog, such talk is mere incantation, the magic of "rationality" (*Vernunft*). One is reminded of Georg Bende-mann's grasping at such straws as his identity crumbles. Gregor, how-ever, has a more frankly magical option, the option of "peace" (*Ruhe*), which has an unexpected kind of potency:

> And for a little while he lay quiet, breathing lightly, as if per-haps expecting such complete repose to restore all things to their real and normal condition.[7]

On a superficial level, of course, this magic is no more effective than the rhetoric of "rationality"; but it is no longer so clear what "normal conditions" are. The peaceful posture does induce a degree of calm in Gregor, the calm of beginning self-acceptance. When he now tries to get out of bed it is "more a game than an effort (mehr ein Spiel als eine Anstrengung)"; and he even "smiles" at the thought of asking for help.

The arrival of the chief clerk (*Prokurist*) puts a temporary end to this. But Gregor's "agitation" (*Erregung*) is succeeded by a new aware-ness of his body as he crashes to the floor. While he continues to respond on a "normal" level, the dimensions of this "new" version of his old life begin to be suggested. The idea crosses his mind that his fate could befall the chief clerk, an idea whose presumption and breadth of perspective would have been inconceivable in his normal state of servitude. And after the mother has sketched his earlier life-style, Gregor reacts with a new calmness, an apparent awareness that, amid the banalities of his family's remarks, he will have to seek the pattern of a past as yet without meaning; carpentry had been his earlier avenue of self-expression, now he will be confined to listening and observing: " 'I'm just coming,' said Gregor slowly and carefully, not moving an inch for fear of losing one word of the conversation." [8] This movement culminates in a resounding "No," wholly natural to Gregor, unbelievable to everyone else.

Once again the movement inwards is reversed, this time by the sister's weeping. In his newly achieved calm Gregor does not understand why she is crying, when he has achieved his own synthesis of "peace" and "rationality": "And it seemed to Gregor that it would be much more sensible to leave him in peace for the present than to trouble him with tears and entreaties." [9] However, his irritable, agitated self-questioning shows that his "No" does not really apply to her, he cannot exclude her. She has reopened the gap between his mental and physical selves which the chief clerk then greatly enlarges. A key to the effect he has on Gregor lies in his appropriation for his own viewpoint of the two attributes with which Gregor has been grappling, restoring them to their old status as clichés: "I thought you were a quiet, dependable person (Ich glaubte Sie als einen ruhigen, vernünftigen Menschen zu kennen ...)." His demolition of Gregor's old identity before Gregor has fully emancipated himself from it causes panic. Gregor's total concentration on the feat of opening the door is not so much an effort to regain his old identity as a desperate urge to be rid of all responsibility for himself.

At the same time, the transformation itself is proceeding uninterrupted, and a strong indication of its "meaning" is offered in the parallel development of self-acceptance in Gregor. The caesura in this first part occurs when the sister departs for help and Gregor realizes his words are no longer understood. With the paragraph beginning "But Gregor was now much calmer (Gregor war aber viel ruhiger geworden)" a new phase opens, in which Gregor's mind is functioning largely on a different level from his body; but as the body's autonomy grows, Gregor's thoughts often seem in a significantly inverse relationship with his actions. Thus it is said of Gregor, "He felt himself drawn once more into the human circle (Er fühlte sich wieder einbezogen in den menschlichen Kreis)," at the moment when the loss of verbal communication entails his definitive exclusion. And yet the feeling is true on other levels: the family, which had previously been fragmented, will now become a unit again in its affliction; and Gregor, through his intense involvement in the trivia of daily life, will become a part of that unit as he never has been as the breadwinner.

When the door is finally opened, Gregor continues to speak as if his old identity were still functioning— but he also feels himself to be "the only one who had attained any composure (der einzige, der die Ruhe bewahrt hatte)." Clearly this speech is different from the earlier panicky outburst, when we were told that he "hardly knew what he was saying (kaum wusste, was er sprach)." Now he is, as it were, speaking experimentally, presenting both his identities simultaneously, the one visually, the other verbally. Moreover, what he says, although in polite terminology, is as open, as aggressive as what the chief clerk had said to him; at the moment of finally losing his old identity, he allows the entire underside to emerge within the framework of an organized personal plea. The chief clerk is right to feel threatened by Gregor. While Gregor's conscious mind persists in developing rationales for his pursuit of the chief clerk, his actions strongly suggest that he is in fact attacking this most resented representative of "the world": "Gregor made a spring, to be as sure as possible of overtaking him (Gregor nahm einen Anlauf, um ihn möglichst sicher einzuholen)." Indeed the imagery of the chief clerk's departure is extraordinarily reminiscent of Georg Bendemann's final moments: "[He] was already ridiculously clinging with both hands to the railing on the landing . . . with his chin on the banister he was taking one last backward look."[10]

But because Gregor cannot communicate, his unleashed aggression appears indiscriminate. The arduous task of controlling his instincts is not yet begun and his involuntary movement in the direction of the spilled coffee makes drastically clear that any literal notion of a "human circle" is illusory. Rejected by both mother and father, Gregor is forced back into himself, both physically and figuratively. At this point the banality of Gregor's mind, the lack of "imagination" which Kobs has shown to be a conscious goal of Kafka's narrative style, begins to acquire thematic force. By doggedly adapting mind to body, Gregor reestablishes the kind of rudimentary communication with the human world that makes a temporary but nonetheless temporal existence possible. That is not to say that Kafka is merely building a naturalistic structure upon an antinaturalist base; Benno von Wiese has pointed to the stylization implicit in the family's behavior:

Significantly, no one around Gregor reflects upon the amazing, inexplicable quality of this transformation. They accept it as a fact, albeit a repulsive one, just as Gregor himself and even the narrator accept it.[11]

The stylized reactions of the family have the same purpose as the transformation itself: to remind the reader that the strict alignment of narrative perspective with Gregor's viewpoint is designed to focus attention exclusively on his responses. All that is arbitrary and undignified in his initial situation becomes, through Gregor's "unimaginative" persistence, the source of dignity, almost of coherence. As in the case of Georg Bendemann, though to very different fictional ends, the "ordinariness" of the hero's thoughts is the necessary modality of an extraordinary mental theater; because of this "The Metamorphosis" has a concreteness of texture that tends to refute Lukacs's fundamental charge against Kafka that his "artistic ingenuity is really directed towards substituting his angst-ridden vision of the world for objective reality."[12]

In the second part the work's central drama is played out. On the one side two forces are ceaselessly driving Gregor towards his death: the trivializing game the sister plays with his existence, which represents an irrevocable denial of his humanity; and the continuing process of Gregor's transformation itself, drawing him ever further into the organic realm, a process his "human" component cannot accept. This conflict manifests itself, almost in passing, in a sentence referring, without further explanation, to Gregor's increasing reluctance to eat: "When he had not eaten, which gradually happened more and more often. . . ."[13] On the other side there is the overt drama of the second part, Gregor's efforts to achieve a modus vivendi. Because the reader sees things from Gregor's perspective he is constantly invited to agree that Gregor's aims are eminently reasonable, perhaps even practicable. At the same time the conclusion of the section, obviously paralleling the conclusion of the first part, introduces an element of ritual that forcibly reminds the reader that Gregor's existence is an impossibility, that the "drama" is only in his mind.

The last speech of Georg Bendemann's father begins: "So now you know what else there was in the world besides yourself; till now you've known only about yourself!"[14] Here lies the significance of Gregor's "inner" transformation; both he and Georg gain this insight only at the cost of definitive exclusion from the human realm, but Gregor has the opportunity, denied to Georg, of rearranging his consciousness. That

Gregor views what lies before him as a form of task is made explicit
at the start of the section: "so he had plenty of time to meditate at his
leisure on how he was to arrange his life afresh." [15] He concludes that
the situation requires "patience and the utmost consideration (Geduld
und grösste Rücksichtnahme)." It is easy to overlook these sentences,
because they sound like mere clichés from the life of a repressed trav-
eling salesman whose past "consideration" has prevented any human
warmth from entering his life. But in context they have a twofold
meaning: Gregor is just learning how to feel "comfortable" (*behaglich*)
in his new body, and such sentiments directly contradict the instinctual
freedom he is now experiencing. The presence of clichés has the same
kind of negative significance as the family's lack of amazement, noted
by Benno von Wiese; it directs the reader's attention to a tenacious
struggle for equilibrium within Gregor. Further, Gregor is now aware
of his family as he had never been while they were his dependents; he
feels "pride" (*Stolz*) at what he has achieved for them and, for perhaps
the only time in his life, asks the kind of ultimate question forced upon
him by his transformation: "But what if all the quiet, the comfort, the
contentment were now to end in horror?" [16] The idea of "patience and
the utmost consideration" is an indirect response to this question. The
ironic opportunity of the transformation is that it has made Gregor
fully "human," aware of the several contexts of his own being. Hitherto
he has "partly lived," his only positive feelings, acceptance and re-
sentment, canceling each other out. Now that communication is impossible, he realizes its paramount importance. He observes his family
intensely, both to enlarge the picture he has of his previous existence
and to glean hints about how he should behave now. Reduced to a
minimal theater of mime, Gregor stakes everything on making com-
prehensible his "good intentions." Georg Bendemann erected the rationalizations of mental theater upon a life of ruthless self-absorption.
Gregor attempts to use the most simplified modes of physical gesture
to impose a human meaning on a body that has its own laws and increasingly insists on following them.

But the static, "experimental" world which both Georg and Gregor
need for the acting-out of their adopted roles is available to neither.
As suggested earlier, two unrelenting forces doom Gregor's efforts to
achieve a modus vivendi: one is his own increasing animality, the other
is embodied in the pivotal character of the sister, Grete. The sister is
seen by Gregor in three different guises, each of them modifying and
calling into question the other two as the story develops. Her reactions
to Gregor are, on the surface, those of an adolescent girl, both intrigued
and repelled by Gregor, eager both to be useful and to explore the un-

known, but above all narcissistic, referring everything to her developing sense of self. But when the reader pieces together hints which
Gregor drops but, because they are irreconcilable with his own enterprise, does not develop, a more complicated picture emerges. The sister is herself experiencing a "transformation," parallel to and in growing
conflict with Gregor's.[17] Stages of this transformation, presented independently of Gregor's perspective, are her hostile "Gregor! (Du,
Gregor!)" at the end of the second part, and her assertion that the
insect cannot be Gregor in the third. At other points the reader identifies himself strictly with the interests of the transformed Gregor; from
this third point of view Grete's personality is nothing more than an in-
strument through which the world rejects Gregor's efforts at self-
adaptation. Put in the form of a theorem, a human being strong enough
to deal with Gregor directly is bound to be insensitive to Gregor's efforts at communication (conversely the person able to "understand"
Gregor, namely the mother, is not strong enough to deal with him
directly). Significantly, the inclinations of Gregor quickly understood
by the sister are purely behavioristic, desires he has made no effort to
communicate: standing by the window and crawling on the walls. The
theorem is graphically demonstrated when the ambivalent sister is supplemented as Gregor's "keeper" by the frankly hostile charwoman.[18]

Gregor's blood tie, his personal limitations, and the imperatives of
the role he is endeavoring to play combine to prevent any of this
from being articulated intellectually; nevertheless, the three elements
in Grete's function rise gradually to the surface of his consciousness.
At first he sees her adolescent character, flighty but benevolent, and
does everything he can to turn her into a permanent channel of communication. From the first a note of impatience is struck, when the
sister's horror at her first glimpse of him makes Gregor half-aware of
her fundamental alienation from him: "well, he had to be somewhere,
he couldn't have flown away, could he? (Gott, er musste doch irgendwo
sein, er hatte doch nicht wegfliegen können)." But at once Gregor
covers up this feeling, emphasizing the positive in the person he realizes
is his only bridge to the world, imputing an elaborate sensitivity to her
brusque gestures:

> And with fine tact, knowing that Gregor would not eat in her
> presence, she withdrew quickly and even turned the key, to let
> him understand that he could take his ease as much as he liked.[19]

Adapting himself to the fact that he will see no one but his sister,
Gregor strains desperately for "a remark which was kindly meant or

could be so interpreted (eine Bemerkung, die freundlich gemeint war oder so gedeutet werden konnte)." It is at this point, while reviewing the shape of his past life, that Gregor reflects, "With his sister alone had he remained intimate (Nur die Schwester war Gregor doch noch nahe geblieben)," and dwells on his plan to send her to the conservatory. Without doubting the "truth" of these intangible thoughts and feelings, one is entitled to see Gregor as to some extent revising the pattern of his past in order to lend meaning to the identity he is now building around his relationship with Grete. Repeatedly the alienness of her attitude becomes abundantly clear to Gregor, as elaborately "considerate" sentence structures are negated by brusquely factual statements:

> She certainly tried to make as light as possible of whatever was disagreeable in her task, and as time went on she succeeded, of course, more and more, but time brought more enlightenment to Gregor too. The very way she came in distressed him.[20]

But having nowhere else to turn, Gregor submerges these painful insights in still more tortuous sentences as he seeks still more extreme ways of effacing, through "consideration" (*Rücksichtnahme*), what cannot be effaced; only the sister's acknowledgment can make these efforts worth while, and so intense is Gregor's longing for it that he can hardly help receiving it, if only in his imagination:

> Had she considered the sheet unnecessary, she would certainly have stripped it off the sofa again, for it was clear enough this curtaining and confining of himself was not likely to conduce to Gregor's comfort, but she left it where it was, and Gregor even fancied that he caught a thankful glance from her eye when he lifted the sheet carefully a very little with his head to see how she was taking the new arrangement.[21]

Gregor's total absorption in the sister's convenience, his desire to accept everything she does as "right" and hence supportive of his identity as a member of the household, leads him to remain passive when she proposes the removal of his furniture.

With the mother's words concerning the furniture we reach the caesura of this central part. Gregor suddenly realizes the falsity of the premise on which he has tried to erect an identity. Within the framework of a single sentence we can see him moving to a new view of the sister: not merely an impulsive adolescent, she is a developing personality whose urge for an identity is fundamentally antagonistic to Gregor's own:

> Another factor might have been also the enthusiastic temperament of an adolescent girl, which seeks to indulge itself at every opportunity and which now tempted Grete to exaggerate the horror of her brother's circumstances in order that she might do all the more for him.[22]

The hopeless contradiction underlying Gregor's efforts is revealed: to fight for his humanness he must behave like an insect. But even as everything is falling apart, dissolving into a struggle for existence Gregor is certain to lose, the worthwhile basis of his "identity" is thrown into striking relief. As Gregor contemplates his intervention, he is conscious only that it must be done "as kindly and cautiously as possible (vorsichtig und möglichst rücksichtsvoll)." When his mother enters, all thoughts vanish from Gregor's mind except the need to spare her the sight of him:

> His mother however was not accustomed to the sight of him; it might sicken her and so in alarm Gregor backed quickly to the other end of the sofa, yet could not prevent the sheet from swaying a little in front.[23]

That Gregor has made "consideration" into his basic impulse, stronger than all his developing animal urges, is clear throughout the dissolution of his tenuous modus vivendi at the end of the second part. His pathetic attempts to assert his rationality, at a moment when it is of no value to him, stand in sharp contrast to the self-centered meanness of the sister and the sheer animal hostility of the father. An enigmatic but much-quoted dictum of Kafka's seems applicable to Gregor at this point, as his identity, cleansed of the self-deception on which it had been built, survives the moment of its destruction: "The light on the grotesquely grimacing retreating face is true, and nothing else."[24] It is paradigmatic for the Kafka hero to glimpse a desired goal at the moment when it is denied him forever; Gregor's goal has been to rejoin his family by literally acting himself, imposing human behavior on an animal form, and the symbolic "complete union (in gänzlicher Vereinigung)" of his mother with his father on his behalf can be seen as the momentary realization of that intimate "human circle" (*Familienkreis*) towards which the transformed Gregor has been striving, but which is in fact a kind of mirage, visible only to him who is excluded from it.

In the third part there is no trace left of the anxious relationship with the sister upon which the central section hinged; for Gregor the sister now is simply the abstract representative of the world which is withdrawing from him. As his family all take jobs, the apartment is filling up with strangers and Gregor's existence has become a fact without meaning. Gregor no longer attempts to unite the human and animal sides of his being, oscillating between unrealistic concern over the family's situation and instinctive rage at the universal inattention to his needs. The only common factor now is the indifference that betokens his coming death: Gregor neither eats anything nor cares at all about the fate of his furniture, which had seemed so vital when the possibility of an identity had not yet been foreclosed. The complete separation of mind and body means that the Gregor of Part Three, while doomed to increasing self-alienation, is also completely "free" in the sense that what remains of his mind, now beyond all responsibilities, is open to the kind of impressions that are normally submerged by the struggle for existence. Gregor himself notes this final stage of his transformation as he begins to respond to the violin:

> He felt hardly any surprise at his growing lack of consideration for the others; there had been a time when he prided himself on being considerate.[25]

Although the premise of Gregor's vision is thus the emancipation of his mind, and the shape of that vision strongly suggests a "fairy tale in reverse" [*Antimärchen*], yet Clemens Heselhaus's formula is not quite fulfilled: "Nature must be destroyed in order that the spiritual can free itself (Die Natur muss vernichtet werden, damit das Geistige frei werde)."[26] For the startling thing about Gregor's "plan" is the degree of self-acceptance it involves. The ambivalence of the rhetorical question "Was he an animal, that music had such an effect upon him? (War er ein Tier, da ihn Musik so ergriff?)" has been noted; the paradox is that only as an animal, indeed only as a mortally wounded animal, are such emotions accessible to him. Gregor has virtually ceased to exist, survived only by a tranquil affirmation of his past in all its aspects. He accepts his physical shape, indeed "his frightful appearance would become, for the first time, useful to him (seine Schreckgestalt sollte ihm zum erstenmal nützlich werden)"; he accepts his mental limitations, salvaging only the plan to send his sister to the conservatory; and he accepts Grete's independence, asking only that she understand him. Gregor does not dream of the reversal of the transformation, only that the barrier of communication that had doomed his rational efforts to achieve an identity be somehow removed. The music makes this seem easy.[27]

If Gregor's words are not taken at face value, a quite different interpretation can be placed upon his vision. But there is every reason to take them at face value. For although Gregor can only achieve these images at an extremity of his life, they do not clash with his common sense, which has by no means deserted him. The striking thing about the very sharp caesura in the third part, which occurs when the lodgers break in upon Gregor's imaginings, is that it does *not* in any way change the direction of Gregor's thoughts. The first sentence about Gregor after the break expresses not confusion but resigned continuity:

> Disappointment at the failure of his plan, perhaps also the weakness arising from extreme hunger, made it impossible for him to move.[28]

By continuing to refer to his vision as a "plan" Gregor stresses its naturalness, its compelling logic as he confronts death. In the vision Gregor affirms the experience of the transformation, pressing it to the point where it would yield a synthesis, his human self turned to the sister, his animal strength unleashed on the "intruders" (*Angreifer*); the image of himself at the center of the family's life is succeeded, as he detaches himself from his body, by the equal and opposite affirmation of what the real sister says—he must disappear. Jürg Schubiger is dissatisfied with Kafka's presentation of death:

> In Georg Bendemann's last words . . . we meet the same banal and unfruitful emotion which also fills the empty, peaceful meditation of the insect before his death. Everywhere Kafka leaves us in the lurch. In none of his works did he portray death believably; when it comes to dying he's not really involved. As a spectator he stands to one side.[29]

The last sentence, to which one can assent, throws into relief the misunderstanding implicit in the remainder of the passage. Kafka's heroes do indeed observe their own deaths. This is because they are always aware of death as something that can be willed, and as the roles they allot themselves in life fail to bring them to their goals, the temptation grows to redeem the whole losing game by a "successful" death. Gregor Samsa in effect experiences his death before actually dying; the word "empty" (*leer*) denotes the willed replacement of his being by the consciousness of his family.

A more serious argument against Gregor's death is the implication in Günther Anders's view that such affirmative emptiness is a dangerous illusion, the slave's acceptance of his slavery:

> Whereas in the history of the emancipation of the individual it was precisely the undetermined psyche, that is, one subject to neither restraints nor controls, that was seen as the essence of being ("being" therefore equals "freedom"), for Kafka only the determined, controlled psyche has "being." [30]

That Kafka was aware of this tendency in his writing is shown by his direct treatment of it in "In the Penal Colony." Here he has embedded Gregor Samsa's death so thoroughly in its context that it is impossible to make an unqualified statement about its meaning—e.g., that Gregor has or has not gained "freedom." This is what troubles Jürg Schubiger: the thematic movements of the story—Gregor's continuous decline from the human to the organic and finally to the inorganic, and the counterpointing transformation of the sister from "a somewhat useless girl (ein etwas nutzloses Mädchen)" to an emblem of self-contained humanity—both are fulfilled by Gregor's death and the family's liberation. And yet both have become encrusted with so much experiential data that a straightforward reaction to the story is no longer possible. The structural simplicity of "The Metamorphosis" demands such a reaction; but the experience of seeing the world from Gregor's viewpoint refutes it, the more so because Gregor's explicit attitude to the world is wholly positive. Thus the moment of Gregor's death epitomizes the complete hollowing-out of his identity, the ultimate working-out of self-negating tendencies already far developed in his life before the transformation; the subsequent emphasis on his shrunken physical shape underlines the finality of his disappearance. At the same time the positive elements inherent in the notion of "living one's life for others" are also brought into the open by the transformation: the dignity of Gregor's doomed struggle for self-adaptation, the self-mythologizing scope of his musical vision, both surpassing and strictly consistent with his life as we have come to know it, finally the conviction that his death will free his family—all this can be seen as an affirmative development, a "raising of the consciousness." A comparable ambivalence pervades the picture of the family after Gregor's death. They have a new self-assurance, an appreciation of life born of genuine suffering, a strength of which they had been unaware throughout Gregor's life. And yet, this independence can be seen as Gregor's final gift to them, anticipated and prepared for by him; moreover, the banality of their aspirations no longer seems convincing after the levels of experience reached by Gregor. Emrich, whose view of Gregor is too tautologous to be very useful—"He can be interpreted only as that which cannot be interpreted (Er ist interpretierbar nur als das Uninterpretierbare)"[31]—accurately conveys the impression left by these final pages:

> When Gregor dies (*krepiert*), the idyllic lie proceeds unimpeded at an intensified level: "three jobs" call them and a marriageable daughter "stretched her young body." The "horrifying end" overwhelmed only Gregor, just because he only wanted to care for his family.[32]

The transformation, by separating Gregor's mind from his body, compels him to act out the personality he had previously taken for granted. In the process that personality comes to seem larger than it ever had been in "life," without losing its inner logic; the banal goal of providing for the family acquires a metaphysical aura—and at the same time the life to which Gregor sacrifices himself is called into question. The logical connection between Kafka's use of the theatrical analogy (here rooted, not in any character's mind but in the story's premise, the transformation itself) and his youthful fascination with the problem of perception is now clear. The fact that we are compelled to view the insect's behavior from both within and without, automatically adding our "objective" image to Gregor's own reasoning, means that a constant process of evaluation is going on in the reader's mind. Is Gregor behaving intelligibly? Is he telling us the whole truth as he sees it? How far is the sister's behavior pardonable? Can we imagine the various scenes ending differently? The simple "inevitability" of the story provokes a constant questioning of all its ingredients until it becomes as enigmatic as the "tree trunks in the snow." The "Play of Gregor," as it might almost be called, dissolves into a series of interdependent layers: the quality of Gregor's life, Gregor's attitude toward his family, the family's attitude toward Gregor, the quality of the family's life. Each layer of the action has a claim to being uppermost in the reader's mind; and each culminates in a parablelike clarity that serves only to generate questions without end.

I have discussed "The Judgment" and "The Metamorphosis" very much in terms of themselves and each other, without ongoing references to my structural thesis. But the heroes of these stories, to a greater extent than elsewhere, come into being through the intimate detail of their stories. To other Kafka characters one can attach at

least one essentially valid abstraction—with Karl Kossman it would be
the theme of "order," with Josef K. that of "innocence"; but with Georg
and Gregor all such abstractions are embedded in the texture of their
lives; their ambitions have no resonance beyond their immediate existence. Only through unprejudiced close reading can the motive force
of these lives, of which the characters themselves are often (sometimes
deliberately) unaware, be isolated and given coherence.

Additionally, there are uniquely private elements in these works
which propel the reader's response into the realm of the psychological.
At this turning point in his career Kafka was utilizing the powerful
emotive connotations of family relationships to produce a central character of "substance"; insubstantiality has, precisely, been both the
theme and the problem of his early writing. By no means does he abandon the achieved tension between hero and world: rather he incorpo-
rates an extra dimension of alienation between hero and reader which
enables "substantial," even irrational aspects of the hero to be evoked
without destroying the dispassionate balance of his art. As the title of
the "breakthrough" story suggests, he wants the reader to *judge* the
hero. If I have seemed to be "for" Gregor and "against" Georg, it is
because the ethical implications of these stories cannot be bypassed.
Without establishing any kind of abstract framework, Kafka is clearly
making use of moral categories to fuel the functional tension between
hero and reader. The hero ignores, misunderstands, or represses a truth
that the reader sees and must respond to. Once Kafka has developed, in
the closed structure, a way of incorporating such tensions into his narrative texture, the reader, while still tempted to "judge" the hero, will
be denied the superior knowledge necessary for success in doing so.

Finally the question of structure. In these stories the two "elements"
are perfectly fused, and hence not prominent as fictional devices. As
my readings have shown, the recreative function of Karl Rossmann as
"author" of his world is developed even further by Georg and Gregor.
Both of them establish mental versions of the world, which they attempt
to defend against the forces of disruption inevitably summoned into
being by their enterprise. At the same time they find themselves cast
in the story's central role, partly through their own volition. Simultaneously they strive to uphold the validity of their fictions and to evade
the logic of their destruction. The outlines of the closed structure are
thus emerging from the open rhythm generated by the authorial hero.
The functional use Kafka makes of family relationships ensured that
the aesthetic balance achieved here could not be repeated. But then,
repetition was something Kafka never sought.

6 Closed Structure: The Trial

"The Judgment" and "The Metamorphosis," the products of Kafka's unique "breakthrough" in the autumn of 1912, are perfectly balanced structures in which the detailing is strictly functional in its alignment with the hero's perspective and also full of independent life, of what Heinz Hillmann calls "pure narrative values (reine Erzählwerte)."[1] This balance is due in part to the very full use Kafka makes of basic family relationships; far from making the stories structural models of Kafka's later works, as Sokel tries to show, the family framework gives them an exceptional flexibility. While channeling everything through the hero's perspective, Kafka utilizes the reader's automatic assumptions about what is "natural" in the feelings of one member of a family for another. Thus in "The Metamorphosis" Grete has a very direct impact on the action without causing the reader to think of her as an autonomous character; her behavior is both suggestive of individuality and, because filtered through Gregor's viewpoint, contained within the archetype "sister" which is partly projected by the reader, partly cultivated by Gregor to protect himself. At the same time the family framework limits the extent to which Kafka can articulate the experience of "angst" in the person of either Georg Bendemann or Gregor Samsa. The last thoughts of both men are for their families; and the radical alienation experienced by them is still an alienation *from* something, from a known, functioning order of things. Although in the last pages of "The Metamorphosis" Kafka implies a continuity of perspective, with the extreme experience of Gregor undermining the "life" that re-emerges after his death, the reader is not compelled to accept this implication; for by tying Gregor's perspective to the family and presenting the transformation as a physical event, Kafka has reinforced the notion that a "normal" world could prevail, that the hero's perspective, to which the reader is restricted, is fundamentally distorted.

The Trial was written two years later, years in which Kafka experienced, through his engagement and especially its dénouement on 22 July 1914, in a Berlin hotel, extremes of self-torture and failures of communication that made the theme of alienation seem both more personal and more universal in its implications. With the emancipation of his hero from the family context Kafka took the essential step towards the creation of a completely closed structure. The characteristics of such a structure can be simply stated in terms of a polarity with the structure of "The Stoker": whereas Karl Rossmann seeks to recreate the myth of order in the world, Josef K. cultivates a fiction of detachment, even disruption, which soon appears more unreal than the "order" confronting him. Where "The Stoker" is essentially linear, opening up new possibilities for the hero in each new situation, *The Trial* is circular, each chapter enacting and confirming the same range of responses in Josef K. to situations that he is allowed to define. In saying this I am merely endorsing what has come to be a consensus of critics about *The Trial.* The basic qualities of the closed structure, which could equally well be called a "created world (geschaffene Welt)" (Martin Walser) or a "subjective world (subjektive Welt)" (Ingeborg Henel), are concisely set out by Fritz Martini:

> Every new confrontation is only a confirmation of the same basic situation . . . It has been rightly pointed out that this repetitive pattern relates to the constructed, "created" quality of Kafka's world, whereas the imitation of an existing world will always be directed at uniqueness and possibilities of change and development . . . . Kafka presents exclusively events of the mind, for which the actual happenings act only as symbols.[2]

The pitfall in this view of *The Trial* is that the critic is led by his perception of the novel's circular structure to neglect the fact that it is a novel, and to reduce it to the more strictly mathematical proportions of a single, endlessly restated parable. Such a reductionist tendency is evident in Walser's original and strikingly paradoxical formulations:

> The fact that the meaning of the work is meaninglessness is not revealed only in the course of the hero's long struggle with his environment; on the contrary, it is already explicitly present in the first occurrence . . . . This eternal circling around the same

point prevents, in Kafka, the emergence of any tension, any
"curiosity concerning the subject matter."[3]

Gesine Frey, who bases her study of time and space in *The Trial* on
Walser's concept of functionality, is concerned that Walser's stress on
the novel's unique structure leads him to overlook its necessary ad-
herence to certain literary norms. Quoting Roman Ingarden, she reminds us that *The Trial* does not exist in a vacuum, that it cannot and
does not neglect the traditional process of building a "world" which is
sufficiently consistent not to require redefinition in every chapter:

> Walser's correct observation that space, in Kafka, is not "em-
> pirical," should not, however, be understood to mean that the
> novel's fictional space is not real within the framework of the
> literary work, and that the apparently real details are only meta-
> phors endowed with the masks of reality. We have already seen
> that exclusively metaphorical literature cannot abide by the
> conventions of fiction.[4]

Gesine Frey's term "quasi-real events (quasiwirkliches Geschehen)"
may seem an inelegant description of the novel's action, but she is
pointing to a very real problem: how does one avoid the "solipsist
fallacy" that, in a closed structure, all events are somehow unreal,
dreamlike projections of the hero's inner desires and fears? The answer lies in the idea of functionality itself: Josef K.'s identity is not
"given," but called into question, simultaneously revealed and de-
molished. This is not to say that Josef K. is in effect nothing, as Beda
Allemann claims, applying reductionist logic to the hero instead of his
environment:

> The reader learns virtually nothing about the inner life of a
> figure, with whose eyes and ears he is nevertheless apparently
> experiencing the world of this novel. Josef K. is nothing but a
> hollow form, perhaps literally nothing but a perspective . . .[5]

Allemann's error is to apply to Kafka a preconceived notion of what
constitutes the "inner life (das Innenleben)," as if "characters" still
existed in the nineteenth-century sense; as we have seen, Kafka's writing, from "Description of a Struggle" onwards, embodies a continuous
questioning and redefining of such concepts. Walter Sokel is more convincing when he talks of the "total ambiguity" of the court facing the

"total ambivalence" of the hero, but in order to decode so "opaque" a text he translates it into psychological allegory, which again does injustice to the restless concreteness of Josef K.'s mental landscape:

> In Josef K., an unacknowledged homo religiosus clashes with the consciousness of economic man. His official impulse of self-preservation and self-assertion resists the upsurge of his unofficial religious impulse, the craving for self-surrender and self-transcendence, objectified by his arrest.[6]

The effect of Gregor Samsa's transformation is paradoxical; Gregor, who had existed rather than lived in the service of his family, is compelled, because his mental dependence is suddenly a physical fact, to reflect on what living for others really means. By acting out, in total isolation, the role he had unthinkingly assumed in life, he endows that life with a kind of dignity. In *The Trial* the theatrical analogy is carried a stage further. Whereas Gregor reenacts a clearly limited emotional life with a single-mindedness imposed by circumstances, Josef K. finds himself in a dialogue with a force that seems designed both to encourage and to frustrate his efforts at self-assertion. The more Josef K. insists on his separateness from the Court, the more intimately do his reactions seem bound up with it; and the roots of this affinity are progressively uncovered during the course of the first chapter, as the contradictions within the two sides are shown to be complementary. The paradox of the Court is simply stated: emblematic of order, hierarchic, and self-contained, it yet manifests itself as a "Störung," an apparent violation of all norms and conventions.

About Josef K., on the other hand, we are told just enough to sense the weakness in his makeup which the Court exploits. He is a creature of regular habits who has achieved a senior position at his bank. In all this he resembles a successful Gregor Samsa, with a conformism untroubled by the gripes of an exploited junior employee (the early sketches for *The Trial* in Kafka's diary have a hero much closer to Gregor's work sphere).[7] But then we are given this curious information about him:

> He had always been inclined to take things easily, to believe in the worst only when the worst happened, to take no care for the morrow even when the outlook was threatening.[8]

This suggests that Josef K. is somewhat detached from his own life, that he goes along with the values of society because he has nothing to put in their place; his escape from the paradox of his own success is to treat his life lightly, to "play" with it by confining himself to the present moment. Now the Josef K. of *The Trial* does not seem very like this: the reader is more inclined to echo Frau Grubach's polar-opposite reaction to him: "Don't take it so much to heart (Nehmen Sie es doch nicht so schwer, Herr K.)." But Kafka uncovers more layers as the unusual passage, in which he stands apart from his hero in the traditional manner, continues:

> ... nevertheless his very first glance at the man Franz had decided him for the time being not to give away any advantage that he might possess over these people.[9]

Josef K.'s decision to behave differently coincides with the beginning of the novel itself: what the reader witnesses, in the continuous, even obsessive unfolding of K.'s thoughts, is in fact a conscious experiment on the part of the character, a deliberate effort to act out the role of a man with a position to defend. Kafka then underlines the unusual mental resolve of Josef K. to draw together experiences from his past, hitherto considered confining: "Though it was not usual with him to learn from experience (ohne dass es sonst seine Gewohnheit gewesen wäre, aus Erfahrungen zu lernen)." The paragraph concludes with a return to Kafka's personal variety of "narrated speech (erlebte Rede)," expressive of the simultaneous alignment with and detachment from his protagonist so ably analyzed by Beda Allemann: "if this was a comedy, he would be a player too (war es eine Komödie, so wollte er mitspielen)."[10] The rule of a confined perspective has been imposed on Kafka by the critics since Friedrich Beissner noticed his use of the technique; but clearly, after the fragmentation of "Description of a Struggle," Kafka is in a position to use whatever technique will best enable him to evoke the enigma of human identity. Here he has chosen to withdraw momentarily from Josef K.'s perceptual range in order to give the reader hints that solidify an impression given by Josef K. from the start of the story: that his strongly worded formulations of his rights and "feelings" are designed to test the responses of the adversary, to afford him an "overview" (*Überblick*) of the total situation that will put the coordinated persona he is presenting in a dominant position in the developing drama.

Josef K.'s strategy depends on the other characters "being themselves," having discernible limitations that he can exploit. But this is where the paradoxes of the situation begin to force him into a state that Sokel rightly calls "total ambivalence." For the strategy of the

Court is to put Josef K. himself "on stage," as the constantly noticed presence of the onlookers in the neighboring building makes plain. When the inspector says, "think more about yourself instead (denken Sie lieber mehr an sich)," he is making explicit the Court's purpose, as far as the reader can perceive it, which is to turn Josef K. inwards, to compel him to give an account of his whole life through his actions in relation to the Court. We thus have a play within a play, and it is unclear to the very end which is "framing" which: Josef K. is forging a persona for himself designed to win the game in which the Court is seen as the adversary; and the Court is constantly providing new stages on which Josef K. is forced to "act" without any clear vision of who the adversary is or how the script should run to his advantage. Josef K. cannot avoid becoming ever more deeply committed to the Court because the "comedy" in which he has decided to "play along" (*mitspielen*) has been initiated by the Court; whether he rejects the role of "arrested person" (*Verhafteter*) or enters into it with a view to establishing his superiority from within, the terms of the play are dictated by the other side and unknown to him. Every time he tries to turn the script in his own direction he finds that everything he says has been anticipated by the Court and merely puts him at a greater disadvantage in the play that is inexorably proceeding.

The paradox within the Court similarly serves to enmesh Josef K. He feels the arrest to be an "intrusion" (*Störung*), and his usual way of life suddenly comes to represent "order" to him. But we have seen how "lightly" Josef K. has regarded the framework of his life hitherto; his concept of order is an assumption rather than a thought-out belief. He is thus vulnerable to the peculiar impact of the Court, which is in notable contrast to its manifestation as "intrusion." Highly organized, it assumes order to reside within itself; so, at the very moment when Josef K. seeks to take his stand on an idea of "order," he is confronted with a phenomenon so obviously "ordered" that it preempts his thoughts on the issue. When Josef K. invokes order in the course of the chapter, he finds that it *includes* the existence of the Court; to his amazement he feels impelled towards "disorderly" rebellious acts, which his rational self at once rejects. The more Josef K. strives to remain detached, like a skilled actor, from the role he is playing, the more he finds that his detachment is merely part of the role as laid out for him by the Court, just as the "interpretations" of "Before the Law" become part of the parable itself. And the more K. tries to anchor his performance to an "objective" value like order, the clearer it becomes that it is too late for him to declare his allegiance to values outside himself; the Court has effectively filled the moral vacuum of his life and dominates thoughts that are nominally in opposition to it. The functionality of this relationship lies in the way both Josef K. and the Court attempt to put together a human identity from opposed points of view. Their efforts are complementary as well as conflicting. As with Gregor Samsa, the process of building-up and destruction is simultaneous, but here there is no physical determinism; Josef K. himself precipitates the confrontations. The more he hardens his posture as the unjustly accused innocent, the more its inefficacy wears him down, until in desperation he tries to wrest from the Court the direction of the only part of the play in which his role is unambiguous—his own death. Ironically, death then becomes ambiguous after all.

Awareness of the novel's theatrical basis allows the reader to observe the actual proportions of *The Trial* instead of picking out "meaningful" passages. As Gesine Frey and others have pointed out, Kafka places great stress on the sheer physical detailing of clothes, furniture, and the grouping of characters: this reflects the priorities (or rather the lack of them) within Josef K., who, caught in the middle of an unreflecting life, tends not to differentiate between the moral and the tangible. Thus before any words have been spoken, there is a lengthy description of the warder's suit, which appears "eminently practical (besonders praktisch)." Even as Josef K. prepares to be outraged by the "intrusion," he is already impressed by the highly "ordered" exterior of the Court. That K. has already taken his decision against a "light" response is shown by his calculating passivity as he "then studied the fellow, silently and carefully, trying to make out who he could be."[11] When he finally does react, his words are ambivalent, the self-righteousness necessary for his role yoked unnaturally, by a revealing "and," to a basic fascination with the intruders which, as he himself realizes—"still, that did not seem important to him at the moment (aber es schien ihm jetzt nicht wichtig)"—suggests a willingness to let them retain the initiative: "I must see what people these are next door, and how Frau Grubach can account to me for such behavior."[12]

From the outset the dialogue is dominated by the physical context, by "scripted" speeches and their counterpoint, unwitting revelation of purpose. In "The Metamorphosis" the impossibility of communication reduced the action to the level of mime, and Kafka has here retained the atmosphere of mime even while restoring speech to primacy as his hero's mode of expression. As the inspector points out after Josef K.'s first statement of his innocence, Josef K. has said nothing that could not be deduced from his manner; but this does not mean his words are superfluous. Although Josef K.'s words never reveal any "truth," neither do they conceal some putative "real self" (the assumption that there is such a thing vitiates, for me, Emrich's whole interpretation). Through his statements in the public realm, Josef K. builds an identity for himself that is neither true nor false, merely tentative; for much of the novel he is aware of its experimental quality, presenting his innocence as a postulate rather than an article of faith. But gradually the gap narrows between his consciousness and his public role, until, on hearing the parable "Before the Law" his identification with the "man from the country (Mann vom Lande)" is immediate and instinctive. But the gap cannot be finally closed: "it was not his final judgment (sein Endurteil war es nicht)." In choosing death Josef K. hopes, like Georg Bendemann, to achieve a "final judgment" by canceling his adopted role and endorsing what he takes to be his adversary's view; but the final outbreak of unresolved questions shows that self-rejection is no more a way to truth than insistent self-affirmation. The quest for identity, for the "clarity" (*Klarheit*) which the manipulative powers of language continually seem to promise, culminates in a total divorce of mind and body far more discordant than the relatively serene self-rejection of Gregor Samsa.

The plunge at the end of *The Trial* from reaffirmation to rejection of an adopted identity is embryonically present at the beginning in K.'s oscillation, partly experimental, partly involuntary, between acceptance and rejection of his arrest (the involuntary element stemming, as we have seen, from the Court's blocking of all the mental exits). When K. first emerges from his room we are told that he moved "as if wrenching himself away from the two men (machte eine Bewegung, als reisse er sich von den zwei Männern los)"; but when told of his arrest he is neither surprised nor hostile, but neutrally inquiring: "So it seems . . . But what for? (Es sieht so aus . . . Und warum denn?)" The arrest is, in this minimal sense, welcomed as a hard fact upon which he must base his role; and the minimal commitment to the arrest becomes sufficient to undermine all opposing self-assertions. This scene is then replayed a few minutes later when K. reemerges from his room, armed with his papers and having made the crucial decision to "play along" (*mitspielen*). The papers formalize his ambivalent posture, their verbal order laying the foundation of the public identity Josef K. is seeking to establish: producing them is an implicit acknowledgment of the Court's legitimacy as well as a defiant act. Gone is the relative simplicity of "But what for?" This time, when told that he is arrested, K. responds: "But how can I be under arrest: And particularly in such a fashion? (Wie kann ich denn verhaftet sein? Und gar auf diese Weise?)"[13] The "manner" of his arrest is thus both the evidence for its factuality and the proof of its impossibility. Similarly, the simple

gesture of revulsion from the warders is transmuted into a complex
combination of verbal aggression with an aloof, tactical involvement:
" '[The law] probably exists nowhere but in your own head,' said K.;
he wanted in some way to enter into the thoughts of the warders . . . " [14]
That this tactical aggressiveness reflects an inability to respond "directly" has already been made clear: "Without wishing it K. found
himself decoyed into an exchange of speaking looks with Franz, none
the less he tapped his papers . . . " [15] Having never functioned without
the props of convention, K. cannot now do so; he has no "self" that
could exist independently of the Court. This explains why K. persists
with his "identity" despite repeated failures, and why he seems so little
concerned with "self-preservation": when he opts, in Titorelli's room,
for total acquittal, he is following the least "safe" course because he is
impelled by the dynamics of his identity, which insists on simultaneous
involvement and independence, accepting the Court's jurisdiction while
rejecting its claim to limit his freedom.

Oscillation between acceptance and rejection, verbal experimenta-
tion and gestural repetition: these are the rhythms underlying K.'s
effort to project an autonomous role in this first chapter. But his attempt to write his own script is doomed because all initiative is in the
hands of the Court; whenever he builds up momentum, he finds that the
Court seems to be monitoring his thoughts as well as his actions, always withholding from him the "overview" (*Überblick*) without which
he cannot master the situation. Walter Benjamin, stressing that in
Kafka's world "man is on the stage from the very beginning," points
out that "whenever figures in the novels have anything to say to K., no
matter how important or surprising it may be, they do so casually and
with the implication that he must really have known it all along." [16]
Whereas Gregor Samsa has to contend only with the strictly logical
consequences of the transformation, Josef K. finds that all his responses,
however "normal," are reduced to schematic fragments of the Court's
preordained script. All his words and gestures instantly become suspended in an analytic vacuum, subject to review by himself, by the
Court, and by the reader. Gregor's one asset, continuity of context, is
denied to Josef K.

In the central scene with the Inspector, Josef K. has been reproached
for concerning himself with such "trivial" matters as the warders' lack
of uniform. But the Court is at once with him in focusing attention on
the details of the scene and the response they provoke in K., on "your
reactions (wie Sie es aufgenommen haben)," as the Inspector puts it.
The warders set the tone by insisting that K. dress for the interview;
K.'s reaction—"Let me alone, damn you! (Lasst mich, zum Teufel!)"

—is a residual manifestation of his initial "everyman" qualities, of the undifferentiated spontaneity that could produce the question "But what for?" At once the warders remind him of the "comedy" that binds him to them:

> "That can't be helped," said the warders, who as soon as K. raised his voice always grew quite calm, indeed almost melancholy, and thus contrived to confuse him or to some extent bring him to his senses.[17]

The paradoxical combination of confusion and "bringing to his senses" (*Besinnung*) embodies the Court's "game plan": by confronting K. with the unexpected, by generating a response and then constantly interrupting that response, they force him away from the general to the particular, to the immediacy of his actual situation. Whereas in the open structure the hero's urge towards an abstract version of his world is continually thwarted, the hero of the closed structure cannot evade the transformation of detail into threatening abstraction. But K.'s commitment to his "identity" as opposed to any principle of order ensures that the "analysis" he applies to his situation belies its abstract phraseology, dissolving into unfocused fragments. As K. by definition lacks the "overview" possessed by the Court he tends to rationalize what is happening to him, mentally transmuting the ever-shrinking scope of action or reaction available to him into a token of his effectiveness, evidence that he has at last drawn the adversary onto his "own" ground. All this is apparent in the Ionesco-like absurdities of K.'s dressing for the interview, a foreshortened summary of the interview itself. Having been "brought to his senses," K. cooperates in picking out his clothes, while ostentatiously remaining "detached": " 'Silly formalities!' he growled ('Lächerliche Zeremonien!' brummte er noch . . .)." When his choice is rejected, we see how K.'s concept of "order" has been preempted by the Court; he can only protest from a point of view identical to the Court's, aligning his own role with the one assigned to him—the arrested man craving only total propriety in his manner of cooperation: "Thereupon K. flung the coat on the floor and said—: he did not know himself in what sense he meant the words— 'But this isn't the main hearing yet.' "[18] From this point his "identity" is wholly internalized, attaching itself to the fantasy that by cooperating he is somehow hastening the "end" of the episode. K.'s very intentness on his own "independence" conceals from him the fact that he is following his adversary's script. The final absurdity is his zealous application of "overview" to what is entirely his own fantasy, the notion that he has cleverly avoided being compelled to bathe: "He kept an eye on them to see if they would remember [the bath], but of course it never occurred to them . . . "[19] This use of "of course" (*natürlich*) would seem to be a conscious breach of Josef K.'s perspective, withdrawing the camera, as it were, to expose the obsessiveness of K.'s retreat, not merely into the details of the situation but into wholly imaginary details furnished to rescue his "identity" from a final merger with the Court's script.

This retreat into fantasy suggests the disintegration under way in K.'s attitude to the Court. When he decided to "participate," the irrationality of the situation was clear to him, the role of affronted innocence seemed uncomplicated. Now the details of the situation have combined with the firmness of the warders to undermine his sense of priorities. Despite his anticipation of the interview with the Inspector, K. is after all unprepared; seeking to integrate all the details of the scene in a single "overview," K. achieves only the dangerous vulnerability of a "distracted gaze (zerstreute Blicke)."[20] The Inspector then begins, on a more sophisticated level, the process initiated by the warders of "confusing" K. by insistently querying him about his specific reactions to the arrest. As K. strives to base his role upon the rational middle ground ("Certainly, I am surprised, but I am by no means very much surprised.")[21] the Inspector dislodges him from it by treating each statement as if he were an anthropologist taking notes. At this crucial moment several processes can be seen at work in K. Partly because of the Inspector's prodding, partly because of his original intentions, partly because of the autonomy of his own language (the obsessive play with the word "surprise" propels K. into calling the arrest first a "joke," then an "affair of no great importance"), he finds himself precipitated into making a formal statement of opposition. As he is about to do so he tries to escape the Inspector's analytic responses by consciously placing himself "on stage": "turning to everybody there —he wanted to bring in three young men standing beside the photographs as well."[22] But hardly has he made his declaration of innocence than he passes immediately to tactical, tangible questions about his adversary, thereby demonstrating his dependence on the Court at the moment when he is supposedly asserting his autonomy—for the warders have already made it clear that the questions he asks will not be answered. Indeed the graceful conclusion to his speech, from the flattening questions about uniforms through the demand for "a clear answer" (*Klarheit*) to the hope for "a parting on the best of terms (den herzlichsten Abschied)," suggests that K. has designed his "public" identity not to be effective but to fulfill a formulaic, almost aesthetic notion of what an identity should be.

If "Before the Law" can be legitimately seen as a distillation of the whole novel, then this exchange with the Inspector parallels the moment when the man from the country decides to wait for permission instead of entering the law. The essential common features are: acceptance of the opponent's legitimacy; withdrawal from actual confrontation to an inner battlefield where tactics can be perfected in narcissistic isolation; and, above all, de facto loss of freedom—without acknowledging what has happened, K. has nevertheless committed himself to a public role which imprisons his responses, sentencing him to endless repetition instead of development and inducing the formulaic quality in *The Trial* which Walser has termed "the shape of the void" (*Leerform*). Analogous to the decisive part played by the doorkeeper's attitude is the Inspector's dismissal of K.'s entire speech, which is the most refined expression of the Court's method of simultaneously "confusing" K. and reminding him of himself. By removing his words from the flow of effective life, the Inspector holds them up before K., so that they acquire an independent "reality" for him, become in the fullest sense his identity, which he immediately sets about justifying and reinforcing. His aggressive dialectic is now viewed as "frankness" (*Offenheit*); his tactical movement from the assertion of innocence to the credentials of his opponents is now presented as a balanced inquiry "about the cause of his arrest and about its instigator (über den Grund seiner Verhaftung und über deren Auftraggeber)." In his "agitation" (*Aufregung*) Josef K. sees repetition as the obvious move; so well-articulated a position must somehow have been obscured by the circumstances of its presentation. Thus he begins the replaying of his role by an attack on the intrusive "audience" in the building opposite: "Officious, inconsiderate wretches! (Zudringliche, rücksichtslose Leute!)" The analogy with "Before the Law" again imposes itself, as K. anxiously studies the Inspector's reaction; indeed a parabolic element enters the narrative itself when Kafka shifts slightly away from K.'s perspective to underline the Inspector's impenetrability: "The Inspector was possibly of the same mind, K. fancied, as far as he could tell from a hasty side-glance. But it was equally possible that the Inspector had not even been listening . . . . "[23] Faced with this enigma, K. accentuates both his aggressiveness, questioning the legitimacy of the whole scene, and his attempt to fulfill the formula of his identity through a handshake.[24] The strictly private quality of this most public gesture is at once evident; the Inspector has made it abundantly clear that his role is not decisive, that any number of handshakes would leave the basic situation unaffected. His refusal to respond, like his analytic rejection of K.'s first speech, merely reinforces K.'s isolation, impelling him to refine and rehearse his role in the hope that the apocalyptic combination of aggression and reconciliation can be successfully acted out.

In later chapters, perhaps most clearly in the interrogation scene, it becomes apparent that K.'s ambition is to play his role to a successful conclusion rather than to achieve advantage for himself. The remainder of the first chapter elaborates the paradox underlying this posture; in opposition to the Court but accepting its framework, K. seeks outside help and understanding but nullifies all help that is offered by vaunting his position as an "insider." In other words, "confusion" and self-awareness, ineffectiveness and self-confidence advance together in Josef K. This is apparent as the Inspector is leaving. The mere alteration in physical circumstances makes K. feel "more and more independent of all these people (immer unabhängiger von allen diesen Leuten)." But this is not the same as feeling free; on the contrary, K. is wholly enmeshed in the role he has adopted, the difference being that suddenly he has the illusion of possessing "overview," the ability to dominate the other characters on the stage: "He was playing with them. He considered the idea of running after them to the front door as they left and challenging them to take him prisoner."[25] As he attempts to crowd the Inspector physically while picking on each of his responses like a hostile trial lawyer, he is imitating, in an exaggerated way, the technique the Inspector has already applied to him. When the Inspector says, "As you are such a quibbler over words . . . (Da Sie auf alle Worte aufpassen . . .)," he could be referring to his own toying with K.'s words at the outset of the interview. The difference, of course, is that K. does not have "overview," that he is playing to the rules of a game he can never control: the Inspector pushes over K.'s verbal house of cards simply by pointing to the bank employees K. has failed to recognize, and then by slipping away unnoticed.

K's reactions show his commitment to the role he has embarked on, his persistence in the struggle for "overview":

> . . . they were subordinate employees of the Bank all the same. How could he have failed to notice that? . . . That did not show much presence of mind, and K. resolved to observe himself more closely in this respect.[26]

But the conclusion of the scene, as K. and the three bank employees leave in the car, shows the true extent of K.'s mental dependence on the Court, with its suggestion of puppet-like motion:

> Yet in spite of himself he turned round and craned from the back of the car to see if he could perhaps catch sight of the Inspector and the warders. But he immediately turned away again . . .[27]

K.'s world is now dominated by the Court; he constantly summons the three employees to his office, "with no other purpose than to observe them (zu keinem andern Zweck, als um sie zu beobachten)." In a revealing fragment this process is carried even further, showing how "being brought to his senses," far from freeing him, only reinforces his determination to control the situation through "overview"; at the same time his acceptance of the Court's legitimacy denies him the basis of discrimination between fact and fantasy:

> The thought that by doing this he was perhaps making it easier for them to keep his own person under observation, which they had possibly been instructed to do, seemed to him such a ludicrous notion, that he buried his head in his hands and remained like that for several minutes in order to come to his senses. "A few more ideas like that," he said to himself, "and you really will go mad." Then he raised his rather grating voice all the louder.[28]

In the scene with Frau Grubach, Josef K. tries to recover the "order" of his previous existence; but it is quickly apparent that the Court no longer needs to be physically present in order to infiltrate every detail of his world. The reader is left in as much doubt as K. as to what Frau Grubach knows of the Court. But for K., her calm reaction is as unnatural as a hysterical one would have been; her ordered existence no longer signifies "order" to him and he begins to enact his role for the third time. At once the solipsistic, obsessive quality of K.'s "identity" is revealed as his dialectic endeavors to transform "something learned (etwas Gelehrtes)" into "nothing" (*nichts*). His reasoning cannot survive even on a theoretical level: "nothing" becomes not only "something," but "all this" (*alles*): "If I had behaved sensibly, nothing further would have happened, all this would have been nipped in the bud."[29] Once again K. turns to particularity and to repetition, attempting to conclude his scene with another handshake; tensely he wonders if Frau Grubach will respond, although such a handshake could mean nothing to anyone but K., fulfilling his "aesthetic" view of himself. But K. now sees disorder everywhere, or rather the "order" of the Court which he cannot help but affirm. Gesine Frey remarks of the bolsters in Fräulein Bürstner's bed as K. now sees them:

> In the context of the bare descriptions, avoiding all superlatives, to be found elsewhere in the chapter, this image has the force of a dreamlike vision in which things alter their proportions disturbingly.[30]

K.'s final rejection of Frau Grubach, and therewith of his whole previous existence, is in fact provoked by himself. When he says of Fräulein Bürstner's late nights, "but it can go too far (es kann aber zu weit gehen)," Frau Grubach regards it as an invitation to some not particularly malicious gossip about her tenant. K.'s furious assertion that she had misunderstood him is in itself dubious (what then had he meant?) and includes a gratuitous untruth ("I know Fräulein Bürstner very well [ich kenne das Fräulein sehr gut]"); when he goes on to rage against her conventional use of the term "respectable" (*rein*, originally meaning "pure"), he is both identifying himself with the "impurity" conferred on him by his arrested status and adopting a domineering tone that meaninglessly imitates the stance of his adversary, the Court.

This attitude is carried over into the scene with Fräulein Bürstner, to whom K. acknowledges a certain amount of guilt, a certain amount of complicity in disorder, as if in search of some middle ground in which to root his "identity": "This morning your room was thrown into some slight confusion and the fault was mine in a certain sense . . ."[31] Influenced by Frau Grubach's gossip, K. is hoping that Fräulein Bürstner may hold the key to a world that is neither the Court's nor the bank's, where problems of guilt and innocence dissolve in penumbra. But in fact, and this is a prime illustration of the novel's functionality, of the systematic yet wholly "natural" denial of K.'s expectations, Fräulein Bürstner's responses remain obstinately within the "normal" framework K. is leaving behind him. If she is involved with the Court, and it is lightly hinted that she is, her role clearly consists of appearing not to have a role. Her straightforward attitude frustrates K., for whom nothing is straightforward; gradually his reactions begin to polarize into the familiar contours of his "identity" with its twin drives towards domination and assertion of innocence: "The Court of Inquiry might have discovered that I am innocent or at least not as guilty as they had assumed."[32] Fräulein Bürstner's response—"Certainly, that is possible

(Gewiss, das kann sein)"—does not satisfy K., who is moving into his paradoxical state of oneness with the Court he is nominally rejecting: "You see . . . you haven't much experience in legal matters (Sehen Sie . . . Sie haben nicht viel Erfahrung in Gerichtssachen)." As K.'s ambivalence becomes clear, Fräulein Bürstner symbolically moves away from the photographs, "where they had been standing together for a long time (wo sie so lange vereinigt gestanden hatten)"; and at the point when, equally symbolically, she invites him to act out the morning's events, he has entered fully into his aggressive "identity" and finds in her, after so many failures, the perfect object on which to demonstrate the effectiveness of that identity. To see the whole scene as planned by K. to this end is to read it backwards and neglect the nuances of K.'s mental movements that make his behavior intelligible, not just schematically brutish. K. is in the "swamp world" (*Schlammwelt*), but he is not of it.

Gesine Frey evokes the complexity of levels involved in K.'s acting-out of the morning's events:

> The scene is truly a play within the play; it develops, as we saw, from a strategy of deception. But as he acts it out K. gradually becomes serious and enters wholly into its spirit. But with the attempt to stage the real event, namely the arrest, by calling out his name, the fictional framework shatters—the call thrusts itself out of the comedy into reality and is answered, on this level, by the captain's knocking.[33]

I would take issue only with her notion that the scene culminates in the reentry into "reality"; apart from the problems of attaching meaning to such a concept in the context of *The Trial*, K.'s shout and the captain's knock seem to me to be events pointing in the opposite direction from "reality." K. is not "really" acting out the morning's interview (the Inspector did not actually "shout" his name);[34] his use of the theatrical mode is propelling him into the private theater of his own "identity," his calling out is a summons to "himself." Similarly, the captain's knock is less a protest from an aggrieved real world than a new development of the Court's basic technique, confusing K. while "bringing him to his senses," K.'s response follows the pattern of the morning's scene; declaring, "I'll put everything right (ich werde alles in Ordnung bringen)," he embarks on words and acts that remind one forcibly, in their self-contained, unrealistic "realism," of his speeches leading up to the demand for a handshake. His kissing of Fräulein Bürstner, for example, is not really directed towards sexual fulfillment;

rather, it is an act of symbolic domination, a banal fulfillment of the "situation" required by the role into which he has fully entered. He is much more interested in having it "said" that he has attacked her than in actually doing so; and his exultant fantasies about Frau Grubach's enslavement completely abandon the human realm (as Fräulein Bürstner makes clear), glorying in the imagined achievement of "overview," of a stage director's control over all possible moves: "If you want to have it announced that I assaulted you, then Frau Grubach will be informed accordingly and she will believe it without losing her confidence in me, she's so devoted to me."[35]

Nothing can stop K. now; the conclusion of the scene, showing so plainly that he has lost all possibility of an alliance with Fräulein Bürstner, illuminates both his adoption of the Court's standards and his inadequacy when judged by them. He has turned his back definitively on the fragile "order" of his previous life, feeling no remorse at his treatment of Fräulein Bürstner. But even as he revels in the "satisfaction" of having acted out his role to its conclusion, he is uncomfortably aware that the scope of his identity has shrunk rather than expanded with his unreserved acceptance of that role. Not only is his "domination" of Fräulein Bürstner without any consequence beyond these few fleeting seconds, but also his lack of "overview" is already clear to him as he worries about what the captain may do. The ambivalence of K.'s role has only deepened with his entry into the "swamp world"; his identity continues to be rooted in his assertion of innocence, but now that innocence has no connection with any "spontaneous" feeling in K. It has become a tactical weapon and as such a necessarily weak and paradoxical one. As K. leaves the world of clear outlines evoked by Fräulein Bürstner, the only world where "innocence" has meaning, he is nevertheless unable to enter fully into the world of the Court. He is condemned to replay endlessly a role that projects both an impossible innocence and an impossible mastery of the conditions of his life. The more fully he enters into the "public" realm to which he now belongs, the more inexorably is he driven back into the awareness that his deliberate solipsism has left him no reality but death.

The closed structure is built upon complementarity: every element in K.'s environment, including the seemingly independent and antithetical Fräulein Bürstner, serves to define his "character," that is, his growing absorption in the identity which he is rehearsing and repeatedly enacting. K. does not "know himself"; indeed he knows less and less about himself as the novel goes on and the responses of his identity become almost automatic and independent of his volition (this is especially vivid in the context of "Before the Law," where K.'s identification

with the man from the country is preceded by no "intellectual" consideration; partisanship is all he knows).

This method of presenting a human existence in all its ambivalent
clarity shows the consistency of Kafka's aim since "Description of a
Struggle." There his twin concerns were for the ambiguity of perception, the simultaneity of "something" and "nothing," and for the
question of human identity, of whether it is "possible to live." These
concerns remain unchanged throughout his life, but through the development of the theatrical analogy in fiction, and then its fulfillment
in the closed structure, Kafka combines them into a single literary
nexus. In "The Metamorphosis" Kafka simultaneously suspends "real"
categories, by presupposing the possibility of human consciousness in
insect form, and insists on maintaining them; thus he can display with
total "logic" the expansion of Gregor's outlook in his physical confinement. And by juxtaposing Gregor's "revelation" through the violin
playing and his shriveled and dirty corpse, Kafka forces the notion of
"identity" into the paradoxical framework of the "tree trunks in the
snow." A human identity is only real when it is also its antithesis. The
closed structure represents a step beyond the strictly experimental,
parabolic form of "The Metamorphosis." The theatrical analogy now
pervades every detail. Josef K. is placed "on stage" by the Court, complete with onlookers across the street; this leads him to embark on a
"comedy" of his own, avoiding the examination of his life by adopting
an aggressive persona designed to capture the initiative and thereby
the "stage direction" for himself. The reader thus sees everything under
a dual aspect: he sees the "facts" as registered by K.'s intellect and then
as transmuted to serve the purposes of K.'s identity. A third layer is
added through the Court's reaction to K.'s behavior, which is close to
the reader's reaction but not identical with it and is in any case at once
turned into material for new calculations by the hero. The fixed nature
of this identity renders it perceptible through the varied detailing of
each context, like the unchanging roots sustaining the tree trunks. But
the image can be reversed; in its total ineffectiveness, K.'s "identity"
resembles the constantly melting snow that covers and re-covers the
same tree. Viewing the action from K.'s perspective, we see it as a
series of testing decisions. But at a slight distance nothing at all happens: except for the arrest and the execution, K.'s existence has no
impact on the Court and the people he importunes. "The Court wants
nothing from you. It receives you when you come and it dismisses you
when you go."[36] This combination of rigidity and fluidity marks *The
Trial* as the fulfillment of Kafka's early ambitions as well as the premise
of all that followed. The traditional topos of the world as a stage is

8 The Functional and the Arbitrary: "The Village Schoolteacher" and "The Great Wall of China"

Walter Sokel sees in "The Judgment" a paradigmatic pattern reflected in all Kafka's later works: an archetypal struggle between father and son acted out through a constantly reappearing triangle of relationships. For all the convincing analogies Sokel finds in the later works, his exegesis of the structural ground plan becomes increasingly rigid and strained. This is because Kafka, when he began to write again after the fulfillment of the closed structure exemplified by the works of 1914, built his narratives on a new set of assumptions, assumptions no longer reflecting the intimacies and inevitabilities of the original familial pattern.

I have frequently used the word "functional" to describe the interlocking details of the closed structure. For an understanding of the basis of Kafka's later writing the same word is called for, but in a more literal sense: the hero of a Kafka story after 1914 defines himself by means of his function within society. Whereas Josef K.'s job in a bank plays little role in his quest for definition (indeed the quest gradually subverts all his interest in his work), the country doctor is a doctor from beginning to end, referring everything that happens to him to his self-image as a doctor. The later Kafka hero is restricted a priori in his responses to events: this is obviously true of K. in *The Castle*, who is much less ready to talk in the abstract terminology frequently favored by the hero of *The Trial*; K. defines himself as a land surveyor and reduces all discussion to the politics of his claim. The later Kafka hero thus implicates a whole society in his existence. As the narrator begins to talk he brings into being a social structure to which he has willed a relationship but which persistently eludes the coherence he attempts to impose on it; the blurring between subjective and objective dimensions so essential to the atmosphere of *The Trial* no longer serves Kafka's purpose. An essential corollary to the Kafka hero's self-definition in terms of social function is that this function is not inherent in his being, in the sense that Georg Bendemann cannot avoid being his father's son and Josef K. cannot avoid the "guilt" that has attracted the Court's attention in the first place. The later hero *chooses* to be what he is, and the arbitrary nature of his choice resounds through the story he tells. One cannot conceive of the man from the country turning around and going home: his involvement with the Law is the very premise of the parable "Before the Law." But in the later works "going away," renouncing his task, is a possibility constantly entertained by the narrator, and the reader always feels it to be a real possibility, albeit one with awesome implications. For just as the narrator, by beginning his story, brings a whole society into being, so, by changing direction or even laying down his pen, he can transform or even eliminate that society. Although this may seem overstated in connection with some of the later stories, the interaction of the functional and the arbitrary in the narrator's relation to his world underlies Kafka's increasing concern with the legends of the past, as well as his own attempts to create "legends" like that of Josefine, the singer. Moreover, the critics[1] who see K.'s role in *The Castle* as that of a messiah come to give life to a sterile society have understood an important dimension of the novel; however lacking K. may be in all the qualities of definition and integrity necessary for a savior, the inhabitants of the Castle world seem aware that without K.'s disruptive persistence their closed world would relapse into a meaninglessness amounting almost to nonexistence. The precarious mutual dependence of narrator and story, function and society, provides the key to Kafka's later development of the idea of the fictional hero, an idea incorporating and refining the aspirations of Karl Rossmann.

The implications of this change of direction for the theatrical analogy underlying Kafka's method are considerable. In earlier works the opening sentences suggested what was to come; elaborate structures enclosing the hero's alienation in a web of symbolic and speculative relationships, they open up the rifts between author and hero, hero and reader, hero and world which are immediately papered over by the rigorous insistence on the hero's perspective. The tension of the closed structure lies in the rival versions of reality, the self-serving mental theater of the

hero, and the invariable, almost indifferent script-writing of his opposition; the end is in the beginning, because the conflict implicit in the
opening words can only culminate in the hero's defeat, the elimination
of at least the most illusory illusion. Whether any kind of "truth"
emerges is quite another question. The closed structure does not develop in any linear sense; it seeks only self-reduction, the forcible elimination of the illusions it has itself generated. "In the Penal Colony" is
both the most austere and most complex example of its kind, counterpointing no fewer than three attempts to contain events in a preordained
script, the officer's, the explorer's—and the machine's own, which nullifies the other two versions without in any way deciding the issues between them.

The machine's enigmatic self-destruction, replacing ideology and
passion with an inexplicable fact, suggests the starting point of Kafka's
later writing. The basic pattern becomes an investigation of apparently
unassailable facts to see whether they will yield any meaning, even the
minimal meaning of their own persisting factuality. Kafka's altered
focus is indicated by a shift in the position of the "implied author," to
use Wayne Booth's term. The key to the closed structure was a quasi-
Flaubertian "objectivity" resulting paradoxically in an elusive, suggestive texture; the restricted perspective led to an oscillation in the
reader's apprehension of the narrative, between an impression of dreamlike solipsism and one of dry, ineluctable "otherness." The oscillation
ceases only in a simultaneity of catastrophe and question mark, which
leaves the reader uncertain as to *what* reality he has perceived but
convinced that he has witnessed *some* reality, indeed, a level of "truth"
surpassing that of most other literature. In Kafka's later works, however, the position of the "implied author" is much less ambiguous.
First-person narration becomes more common, and the reader feels
that the concerns of narrator and author are identical, that all cards are
being put on the table. The new paradox is that unmediated focusing
on the "facts" of a story results in a dialectical calling into question of
both the narrator and his world, so that the reader comes to feel, despite the narrator's openness, that he has witnessed only an *absence* of
reality, a narrative running into the sands of language without content.

The situation can be illustrated by a comparison with a remarkable
children's book, *A Picture for Harold's Room*, by Crockett Johnson.
Harold begins to draw a picture which effortlessly achieves a reality
into which he can enter; initially he is a giant and controls everything,
but gradually his enthusiasm for drawing becomes autonomous until
he suddenly discovers that he has created a gigantic, threatening world
populated by outsize flowers and mice towering over him. To regain his

equilibrium Harold simply declares that it is all just a picture and steps out of it.[2] The Kafka narrator similarly begins by evoking a world in which his own function is at one with the natural order of things. But as he subjects this order to questions that at the beginning seem inconsequential, he finds himself gradually moving into a position where, like Harold, he must either declare his whole world to be arbitrary or, by withdrawing from it, call into question the functional basis of his own existence. Kafka is moving towards the characteristically modern literary situation in which the act of narration is itself the primary source of tension. But the mirror-world of Jorge Luis Borges is prevented from emerging here by the insistent limitations of the narrator, his commitment to a function within the world he describes. No longer a character in a play scripted by others, the later Kafka hero is the author of a play in the course of which his own life is to acquire meaning. He cannot write the play without first defining his own role, and he cannot define his role without first writing the play. The ultimate symbol of this paradox is the animal in "The Burrow," who actually completes a world in his own image only to find it defective in virtually every respect. If the closed structure is a cycle of self-generated endings, the structures developed by the later Kafka consist of a series of fragmented beginnings, forestalling silence only by arbitrary acts of will.

Before such generalizations get out of hand (if indeed they have not already done so), I should like to turn to two texts illuminating the genesis and refinement of Kafka's later style, "The Village Schoolteacher"[3] and "The Great Wall of China."

"The Village Schoolteacher," written at the same time as *The Trial* and "In the Penal Colony," during the latter months of 1914, suggests Kafka's changing focus to a remarkable extent. We are told little enough about Josef K.'s personal life, but the multilayered structure of *The Trial*, to say nothing of the fragmentary chapters appended to it, impel the reader to think of Josef K. as a potentially whole being built up through his definitions of himself and those of others. Concerning the narrator of "The Village Schoolteacher," however, information is more rigidly restricted: we know only, from the story's first line, that he is among those who dislike moles, and, much later, in an aside, that he is a merchant. The decisive fact about him is contained entirely in the story itself: his decision to intervene in support of the schoolteacher. The very inexplicability of this decision, its unrelatedness to even the minimal facts we are given about the narrator, is of course the important thing about it. The narrator is defining himself in terms of pure function, creating a role for himself independent not only of any anterior life of his own, but also of any facts outside the story he is now telling.

The mole's unverifiability is not secondary, as he suggests at the outset, but primary in protecting him against the danger threatening all the later Kafka heroes—anonymity. If the mole could enter the realm of fact, then the reasoning the narrator employs to illustrate the likely fate of the schoolteacher's paper would apply a fortiori to himself; nothing could be more anonymous than the supporter of a supporter of an accepted fact.

The seemingly unchallengeable remoteness of his chosen function, however, draws the narrator into the central paradox of the later Kafka: abstract though it be, the function still refers to an objective world, a world containing both the schoolteacher and the people to be converted by the narrator's pamphlet. The narrator makes his impatience with these variables abundantly clear. He is not interested in either the schoolteacher's personal fate or the possibility of actually converting people. But without these minimal connections with an independent world the idea of a function would lose its meaning, and because of them the narrator's function crumbles inexorably into nonexistence while he shifts his ground desperately in an effort to preserve some residual meaning for his undertaking.

As in many later Kafka stories, notably "A Country Doctor," continuity, apparent logical consistency, is imposed on the story by the narrator in order to prevent the undermining of his position from becoming apparent. In this limited sense the act of narration, the transformation of absurdity and weakness into common-sense behavior, becomes intertwined with the narrator's claim to functionality—but by delaying the collapse of his endeavor the stylistic maneuvering only makes the sources of weakness more obvious. The reader can go back and plot the graph of the narrator's failure analytically. Here the narrator begins with the deceptive tranquillity familiar to us from "The Judgment": a common-sense world exists, a rift has opened in it, and the narrator has assumed the task of restoring harmony. As in the case of Georg Bendemann, the narrator's conciliatory efforts culminate in a piece of writing; indeed, the entire story can be read as an adaptation of the theme of "The Judgment" to this narrative rhythm. To employ Wayne Booth's terminology, whereas our interest in Georg Bendemann is "practical," impelling us towards the concrete, even brutal human drama behind the verbal abstractions, our involvement here is "qualitative" and moves us in a reverse direction. Behind the unassuming presentation of the narrator's procedures we sense a "rage for order," an irrational insistence on function as an end in itself. We know no more of the narrator than his decision to enter the schoolmaster's case, but this decision, with all its overtones of the artist's endeavor to impose

a pattern on a recalcitrant world, generates a drama all the more intense
for its narrow scope.

The narrator's insistence on not reading the schoolmaster's paper or
even communicating with him alerts the reader to the absurdity underlying his claim to functionality. Such methodological purity amounts to
a denigration of the subject matter, as the schoolmaster immediately
points out. He is obviously analogous to Georg Bendemann's father as
the "representative of the world," but whereas the father destroys
Georg and allows the possibility of meaning to emerge through the act
of negation, the schoolmaster merely undermines the narrator's pre-
tensions, depriving him of meaning. Kafka expressed this contrast in
an epigram:

> To avoid a semantic confusion: what is to be actively destroyed
> must first have been firmly grasped; what crumbles, crumbles,
> but cannot be destroyed.[4]

Kafka's later style is concerned with crumbling, rather than destroying; here the process is set irresistibly in motion by the schoolteacher's
initial response to the narrator's paper. The narrator's purity of method
could be justified on two grounds: it might succeed in eliminating all
doubts concerning the mole—or it might, through sheer systematic
rigor, at least constitute the last word on the subject. But justification
either by ends or by means is precisely what the schoolteacher denies:
the narrator's paper, in his view, is not only unsystematic, it casts doubt,
because of its differences with the schoolteacher's own paper, on the
very thing it purports to prove, namely, the existence of the mole.

From this point on the original idea of the narrator's function is lost
sight of (the "crumbling" process). This is illustrated by his irritated
assertion that the schoolteacher's paper was itself not at all "credible"
—which, however, does not mean that the narrator is "really" out to
attack the schoolteacher, in the sense that Georg Bendemann's concerns
are masks for aggression against the father. This is the point at which
both the parallels and the differences with "The Judgment" become
more pronounced; as in "The Judgment," writing, the organization of
ideas and emotions into verbal forms, becomes the dominant motif of
the middle of the story (a motif which is itself, as Evelyn Torton Beck
points out, an echo of Yiddish theater practice).[5] But whereas Georg's
letter is merely a weapon in a continuing struggle, a weapon which the
father strips from him, for the narrator here his text is more like a shield,
a protective covering without which he is entirely naked. The rationality
with which he established his function in the first place now works

against him; the flow of thoughts seems to express only the school-teacher's point of view, a view which would demolish his very reason for being. The immediacy and fatefulness of "The Judgment" is absent here, but the sense of a mind losing its own autonomy is even more vivid, perhaps because this autonomy, this capacity to choose freely and meaningfully, is the sole issue at stake. Against the attack on his function the narrator can only set the text of his pamphlet as evidence that the function has already been achieved and cannot be taken from him. But his first quotation, the modest and seemingly unassailable statement of his desire to disappear from the case, is immediately assaulted by the schoolteacher as hypocritical. The narrator retreats still further from his original function, with his statement that the mole's existence is "not completely and irrefutably established (nicht vollständig einwandfrei)"—whereupon the acceleration of the crumbling process is graphically illustrated by the response of the newspaper, the printed word, the context of readers that prevents even the pamphlet from achieving a self-sufficient existence. The confusion of the two pamphlets is an image of anonymity anticipating Kafka's reformulation of the Prometheus legend. The rights and wrongs of the newspaper's error are irrelevant; crucial only is its failure to acknowledge the narrator's existence. Refuted on a rational level by the schoolteacher, the narrator finds the refuge of the autonomous printed word symbolically closed. There is no sense whatever in which his intervention has become functional.

The third and final stage, the confrontation with the teacher, contains many echoes of "The Judgment," notably in the details of the narrator's movements. For example: "He drew the letter a little way from his pocket and let it drop back again" ("The Judgment"); "For the time being I kept my hand over the circular" ("The Village Schoolteacher").[6] The circular referred to is the narrator's final card, a text presented even more elaborately than the pamphlet itself. A not-so-simple request for the return of the original pamphlet, it represents an attempt to forestall the crumbling process by what Kafka, in his epigram, terms "active destruction." The narrator has not managed to achieve recognition of his presence; if he can extract at least an acknowledgment of his withdrawal, then his activity will have achieved functionality, if only at the point of dissolution. But even this is denied. The schoolteacher, in an ironic reprise, presents an image of what the narrator's function might have been—an image totally remote, in its emphasis on joy and humanity, from anything the narrator has conceived. Although the passage evokes alternative worlds it is not, I think, intended as a critique of the narrator's actual behavior, if only because in the presentation of this narrator Kafka does not, as he sometimes does in earlier works, invite consideration of alternatives. Since the narrator has defined himself solely in terms of his arbitrarily assumed function, our interest in his responses, notably his ill-concealed aggressiveness towards the schoolmaster, relates not so much to the narrator as an individual as to a more general theorem of human behavior. Indeed the narrator is "right" in his demolition of the teacher's Utopian hopes: the facts of the human world are as he describes them—but these same facts have already refuted his own claim to a functional existence. The juxtaposition of the schoolteacher's dream with the desolate actuality suggests that the narrator's failure is due not to his mishandling of the situation but rather to the very conception of his undertaking. Function is an abstract idea that cannot be approached abstractly; the only meaningful function available to the narrator in this situation is the one imagined by the schoolteacher, entailing total involvement in the situation, commitment to the cause of the teacher and the mole, unreserved identification of self with social ambience.

Another of Kafka's epigrams is suggestive here: "The word *sein* signifies in German both things: being and belonging."[7] Existence is only possible in the context of "belonging"; if one does not belong, there is no possibility of regaining a social function by an arbitrary act of will. The intimate relation between the functional and the arbitrary in Kafka's later works is predicated on their ultimate incompatibility. The Kafka hero does not merely want to "belong," and much of the difficulty in interpreting *The Castle* has arisen from the assumption that he does; rather, like the narrator of "The Village Schoolteacher" and the animal in "The Burrow," he seeks simultaneous autonomy and involvement, a mental state at once inside and outside his arbitrarily chosen function. As Jörgen Kobs points out, this impossible, circular situation, far removed from the clichés of alienation and the absurd, is embedded in Kafka's sentence structure:

> As long as the mutually limiting sentences circle around each other, the decision between positive meaning and meaninglessness remains in the balance. Such a condition both offers and withholds consolation. At the same time as it prevents the onset of the absurd, it denies, at least insofar as the intelligible content is concerned, any concrete possibility of salvation.[8]

As in the case of "The Burrow," the "fragmentary" ending of "The Village Schoolteacher" is extraordinarily effective. The narrator, having continually sought an abstract relationship with reality, is denied even the option of "destroying" his own function. After all his carefully prepared speeches endeavoring to transform at least this one moment of time into a "text," after repeatedly flourishing the magnanimity of his withdrawal—the schoolmaster just continues to sit there, puffing on his pipe. The scene is as "theatrical," in a different sense, as the conclusion of "The Judgment," with which it invites comparison. The sheer neutrality of the scene, the sudden and definitive swallowing-up of all intellectual patterns into irrefutable, meaningless facts, suggests a theatrical concept so refined that it can dispense with conflicts and "characters" and gain all its drama from the props, the mere existence of a stage. For all Georg Bendemann's self-destructiveness it still makes sense to talk of the father's "victory." Here, in contrast, there is only defeat. The narrator has built his own stage, has drawn his own picture, and has brought into existence a set of minimal facts and relationships which deny him, their creator, any role whatever. The psychic "crumbling" evoked by this scene is perhaps even more devastating than the physical annihilation that concludes "The Judgment."

The mere fact that "The Village Schoolteacher" was composed in the shadow of *The Trial* suggests that there is nothing radically "new" in the actual psychology of this narrator. The movements of his thoughts are similar, in their irrational rationality, to those of earlier Kafka heroes; what is new is the reduction in our knowledge of him and the arbitrary nature of his relationship to society. This enables Kafka, while maintaining a strictly limited perspective, to develop an embryonic "psychology of society" as a force neither intimate nor mysterious which nevertheless seems systematically to deny the narrator's claims. In "The Great Wall of China" (1917) Kafka enhances these novel elements in his narrative perspective as far as is possible without abandoning the governing role of the narrator hero. The narrator of "The Great Wall of China" identifies himself with his society; he does not have any individual aspirations, he is not afraid of anonymity, his functional position in his world is assured. Kafka seems metaphorically to be putting a question ultimately confronted in his last story, "Josefine, the Singer": Is it possible, by placing the narrator inside society and reducing the reader's personal interest in him almost to zero, to understand the rationale and dynamics of society as a whole? Although the logic of Kafka's development impels him to put this question, the accumulated evidence of his writings makes the answer almost inevitable: just as the act of human perception implies an accompanying negation of that perception (an idea discussed at the outset of the chapter on "Description of a Struggle"), so, a fortiori, "society" can only be defined by its conceptual antithesis, the observing individual. "Order" is an attribute of the mind; the observer cannot be eliminated from a portrait of society any more than the "implied author," as Wayne Booth has demonstrated, can be removed from a work of fiction.

Once the individual observer/narrator is posited, however, the epistemological circle begins again. However unassuming the narrator, however conscientious his attempt to see society as a whole, his function as a recorder of facts will push him towards autonomy and isolation; the facts will seem to develop a logical momentum which, once thought through, cannot be unthought. And this logic, as Jörgen Kobs's study shows, moves always in the direction of self-contradiction. "The Great Wall of China" begins and ends on a factual level, the fact of the wall and the fact of the self-contained village life. Although these facts are connected by an unbroken thought sequence, they are basically incompatible. At the beginning the Chinese people are disciplined, unified, and idealistic; at the end they are independent, skeptical, lacking even the impetus towards unity. The narrator shows signs of becoming aware of this paradox in the last paragraph but, understandably, breaks off before tackling it.

The source of the growing meaninglessness of the narrator's undertaking lies in his dual posture. He is in the position coveted by many another Kafka hero, inside and outside society at the same time. But there is no fulfillment: the abstraction of "society" and the actuality of people undermine each other just as surely as if the narrator were personally committed to the abstraction. Indeed in a sense he *is* committed, in that the "idea" of society, if it exists, is inaccessible and his attempts at formulating it, however "objective," are his own and valuable only for being his own. The narrator scurries between his two roles as "man of the people" and "historian." When the wall seems to be becoming too theoretical a fact, he resorts to local color from his own experience, but soon finds himself patiently putting together a new intellectual pattern. The crucial transition comes in the center of the story, when the idea of the wall is developed into a climactic, Kierkegaardian act of faith in the "leadership." At this point, when humanity as the narrator presents it seems willing to accept anonymous fulfillment, the functionality of the narrator reasserts itself. It is not that he is becoming more "personal" than before—on the contrary, the text tends more and more towards the timeless formulation of parable; rather, the simple fact of the narrator's presence precludes the stasis of a fulfilled pattern. He has drawn this picture, which cannot, by definition, be "objective"; he is, as it were, standing there before it, pencil in hand. Behind him is the continuing, unabsorbed reality of the human world. And so, arbitrarily, he begins a new picture, switching from the Protestant, other-worldly idea of the leadership to the Catholic, institutional imagery of the emperor. The two ways of thinking can be seen as an encyclopedic attempt to contain a whole society, but they cannot, without contradiction, both be presented by a single voice. As the narrator moves down again from the transcendental to the popular level, his imagery of privacy and dislocation systematically undermines the theoretical fervor of the first part. Although the narrator retains his impersonality, at the end we can almost visualize him: a puzzled man, confronted by the contradictory logic of his failed enterprise.

From whichever direction meaning is sought, the incompatibility between the arbitrarily human and the self-contained functionality of a society will render it inaccessible. That Kafka continued, despite his own logic, to extract metaphors for meaning from the very process of its fictional destruction, will be the theme of my last two chapters.

9 Reopened Structure: The Castle

"Reopened structure" may seem an odd description of Kafka's elusive, even claustrophobic novel, but when set beside the closed structure achieved in *The Trial*, *The Castle* can be seen to move in a new direction. In the process of perfecting the closed structure Kafka had to abandon that sense of the randomness, the fragmented absurdity of human existence which was so dominant an element in "Description of a Struggle"; in *The Trial* every descriptive detail has a bearing on the relationship between Josef K. and the Court, and the reader quickly becomes aware that in this world nothing is accidental, nothing could happen otherwise. In "The Metamorphosis" Heinz Hillmann can still detect details that are "reine Erzählwerte,"[1] evocative for their own sake; in *The Trial* such detailing is no longer possible. In the years between *The Trial* and *The Castle*, however, as we have seen, Kafka gained a renewed interest in the sheer arbitrariness of life. At the same time his stories, while richer in the purely incidental, aspire increasingly to the texture of parables, illustrations of the teleology of frustration which he elaborated in countless epigrams and fragments. His narrators, striving to bridge the gulf between experience and meaning by means of the idea of function, become puzzled, anonymous observers of their own failure.

In August 1917 Kafka's tuberculosis was diagnosed, a phenomenon which he at once discerned as only nominally physical and very far from arbitrary; and in November 1919 he wrote the long letter to his father in which he seeks to define the whole pattern of his life's failure in terms of the relationship with his father. These two central biographical events, so laden with "determinism," suggest that Kafka found himself rebelling, however negatively, against his own formulations of an arbitrary universe. And his decision to attempt once again the articulation of a novel's self-sufficient world may have resulted from a desire to integrate his renewed interest in a determined "identity" with the parabolic skepticism of his later style.

The image of a land surveyor serves his purpose perfectly. It is the ideal function for a Kafka hero, simultaneously inside and outside society. But like all ideals it cannot be realized. If society accepts the hero, it draws him inwards, canceling the assets of the outsider. If it rejects him, he cannot meaningfully exist, for a surveyor must survey. The fictional balance of *The Castle* depends on a perpetual oscillation between these extremes. The castle neither accepts nor rejects K., compelling him to define his function on his own. Inexorably, K. transforms the potential meaningfulness of his position into its antithesis, being lured inward while striving vainly to remain "outside" when it matters least, "surveying" an ever-narrowing segment of the society he confronts. Whereas in *The Trial* the protagonist found that all "fresh" scenes dissolved into the same confrontation generated by his own "identity," here K.'s frustration stems from his inability to bring his identity into being; a function that presupposes stability is nullified by an incessantly shifting environment. Hints of a rigid spiritual hierarchy (prematurely institutionalized by Max Brod) are offered from such a variety of viewpoints that diffusion of meaning beyond the capacity of any one individual comes to appear as the central purpose of the Castle's bureaucracy.

Martin Walser remarks rightly that the formulaic quality which so well defines *The Trial* is present in *The Castle* in an intensified form:

> The interval between the hero's self-assertion and the negation thereof has become much smaller compared with *America* and *The Trial*. The two movements have coalesced into an almost static consistency, which brings the novel's rhythm to the point of monotony. The individual occurrence is so completely interwoven with its predecessor and with its later repetition that the caesurae merge with one another.[2]

He does not, however, press his dialectic to its logical conclusion: if the formula is so thoroughly integrated with the novel's texture that its outlines have ceased to dominate the reader's consciousness, then the contextual details must be reasserting their primacy—otherwise the novel would be unreadably dry and "monotonous." The details necessarily gain their life from K.'s impact on the world of the Castle, and here the complementarity between hero and environment is as apparent, in a reverse sense, as that to be found in *The Trial*. There both sides enacted a preordained script, talking past each other until the moment of conflict endlessly renewed. Here both sides offer a self-definition in terms of function; the Castle system, with its rigidity and its constant motion, presents a striking contrast to the static, shadowy world of the Court. But just as K.'s assertion that he is a land surveyor never reaches the point of being either proved or disproved, so all the activity of the Castle achieves no goal beyond self-perpetuation. The quest for meaning is mutual: the Castle is a perfectly equipped stage without a principal actor, K. an actor without a stage. This fusion of the problems of identity and function results in detailing entirely unlike that of *The Trial*. There the details accumulate, fall into place; here they cancel each other out or hang in a void, as if anticipating the beginning of the "play" that would give them meaning. It is thus an error to seek to define K.'s "purpose" as if it were distinguishable from the needs of each successive moment.

Emrich simply assumes that K. is in search of an "existence worthy of humanity (menschenwürdiges Dasein)." At the other extreme, Walter Sokel sees him as perpetrating a "colossal fraud," but because emphasis on the apparent disingenuousness of some of K.'s assertions raises an urgent problem of motivation, Sokel has to resort to a priori existentialism:

> Like every man, K., in order to be, has to be recognized and related as an individual to the whole of society; he must have a specific calling. In order to get his call, he must already be someone, an accredited and required expert. However, K. knows he has no call and is, therefore, nothing .... Since a human being cannot live permanently outside humanity, K. desperately needs to enter it, that is, to become someone needed and recognized.[3]

The difficulty with such a view is that it assumes an "inner life" in K. about which we are not told, while ignoring certain awkward facets of K.'s behavior. He is not as consistently accommodating as such "desperate" motivation would require him to be, nor does he always associate his aims explicitly with his "calling" as a surveyor.

Klaus-Peter Philippi makes the illuminating point that K. and the Castle define each other; whereas the basis of *The Trial*, he says, is "impossibility" (*Unmöglichkeit*), that of *The Castle* is "possibilities" (*Möglichkeiten*), and, adapting Walser's phrase, he describes K. as an "empty vessel of possibility (Leerform von Möglichkeit)." In thus stressing the openness, the provisional quality, of everything that happens in *The Castle*, Philippi's book is invaluable. But in searching for "possible" approaches to K., Philippi occasionally crosses the line from flexibility to inconsistency. At one point he says that only K. has a "nature already fixed (vorgeprägte Natur)" and that his task is to "define" the Castle: "K. must replace this world's lack of definition by definitions (K. muss die Unbestimmtheiten dieser Welt durch Bestimmungen ersetzen)."[4] But at a later stage, invoking Sartre's view that man "becomes" through his actions, he suggests that K. is only the "sketch" (*Entwurf*) of a character. Then again, K.'s "Utopian" basis is revealed in his persistent pursuit of a single goal. Taken individually these points are all most suggestive; taken together, they show that Philippi is not strict enough in pursuing his initial insight that Kafka has here articulated a total mutual dependence between hero and environment that systematically preempts the development of meaning.

One of the lessons of Kafka's late works is that there are no "outsiders" a priori, only people who have elected to define themselves as such. The hunger-artist has transformed an entirely negative characteristic, the absence of a desire to eat, into the basis of an outsider's existence; with society's withdrawal he is no longer "outside" anything, but salvages his identity by, on the one hand, acknowledging its fraudulent basis and, on the other, persisting in his decision beyond time and the social context. In *The Castle* Kafka has taken the dual risk of removing the structural definition supplied by a function like fasting while at the same time enlarging his picture of society to suggest self-sufficient characters who yet lack the essential component of meaning. With the elimination of the familial and ethical dimensions so prominent in earlier works, Kafka has both narrowed his focus to the single intellectual pattern of the outsider and society, and also widened his fictional canvas in order to evoke the sheer weight of detail in an arbitrary world, preventing the hero from articulating the pattern he himself proclaims at the outset. On one level the situation is wholly abstract: K. is a "man without qualities," a being without an identity: while the Castle is an organized system of identities which, as many critics have pointed out, is inherently *geistig*, lacking in life. As he has done in earlier works, Kafka simply makes their coming together the premise of the novel, leaving questions like why the Castle exists or why K. has come unanswerable, indeed not worth asking, except insofar as the novel's events offer a retrospective answer. Such an answer is actually implicit in the first paragraph, which dwells on K.'s prolonged contemplation of the invisible Castle: the relationship is already complete in its impossibility—K.'s identity is that of an outsider from a system that automatically excludes him. At the same time K. and the Castle are separated not by an absolute gulf but by an "apparent emptiness (scheinbare Leere)," a phrase pointing to both the deeper complementarity between the two (K. needs an identity, the Castle needs "life") and the temptation held out to K. to abandon his position as absolute outsider and shift to a middle ground.

This middle ground is the mundane world of the characters K. meets in the village. They are limited, on the one hand, by being viewed solely in a functional relationship to K. and, on the other, by their roots, which they often cannot articulate, in the Castle system. But they are not automata: their independent life is essential to Kafka's purpose, which is to suggest the reality of identities already achieved within the orbit of the Castle system and the temptation to K. to seek such an identity for himself. What binds the two levels, the abstract and the worldly, together, is the analogy with the theater underlying K.'s situation. K. is not explicitly on stage, as is the hunger-artist, but the theater, a functional image uniting the concepts of identity and society-as-audience, shapes the novel's structure from the outset, as Bluma Goldstein points out in an unpublished dissertation:

> In the third paragraph it is the narrator who announces that the "play" is beginning—the protagonist is awakened and activity worthy of dialogue commences. The theatrical atmosphere is specific in the description of Schwarzer ... The play is not being performed for K. He is a character, indeed the main character, in the drama, the peasants his audience ... If, before this, K. appeared the stranger, this fact was, in itself, not disturbing for him. However, from the moment he is awakened, the reader is aware that the prologue has been played, the stage has been set and the action is about to unfold. K. too, as has been indicated, is conscious of being involved in a drama .... Kafka initiates the narrative action in abstract terms, that is, within the framework of theatre or drama which normally tends to be more selective and abstract than straightforward narration. The continued and careful realistic description, the objective, almost impassive writing and the sudden suspension of the theatrical image force the reader to accept the reality and verity of events. However, once the sense of strangeness, of distance, of the abstract, have been evoked, they persist throughout.[5]

Two points here are important to my argument: K.'s initial self-acceptance, prior to being awakened by Schwarzer, and the fact that the Castle introduces the theatrical atmosphere. In itself the Castle system is the very antithesis of theater, reducing all life to prose. But when Bürgel reveals that beneath the system's automatic self-perpetuation, the officials sometimes experience the urge towards total dissolution, he makes it clear that dissolution would only follow a specific scenario; a person who had retained his identity as an outsider would ignore the appropriate channels and directly approach an official who is not "competent" (*zuständig*). An arid system would then dissolve in a joyously theatrical moment of life. The Castle, in its self-perpetuating role, fears that K. might be just such an outsider and so, by initiating a scenario of its own that appears to offer a form of acceptance, it aims to prevent the consolidation of his identity as outsider and divert him into the middle ground, the realm of endless "possibilities." Once K. has swallowed the bait and begun to seek "ways" to the Castle through the people in the village, no matter how uncooperative his attitude, the Castle is able to hold him in a state of perpetual oscillation, alternatively luring him inwards and thrusting him back into isolation. Once the assistants arrive in the second chapter, to "entertain" him like jesters at a medieval court, K. in effect abdicates his role as outsider, devoting his energies to gaining mundane successes and discovering who is or is not influential, while the villagers play endlessly on the theme of K.'s insignificance. But throughout the first chapter, with K. still close to his initial independence, things seem more open. The burden of what K. learns from each conversation is that K. is directly—i.e., abstractly—related to the Castle, but that the inhabitants of the village will have nothing to do with such a relationship and, consequently, as little as possible to do with K. The subsequent direction of the novel is determined by K.'s attempt to have it both ways, to combine an abstract mission with functioning personal relationships.

Walser remarks acutely that Josef K.'s declarations of innocence in *The Trial* represent an effort to prevent his trial from getting under way, to stop the play, in effect, before it has begun.[6] In *The Castle*, by contrast, K. willingly casts himself as the central character; repeatedly he initiates conversations with the villagers in the hope of starting the "play" that will lead to a definition of his identity. The reversal of the relationship in *The Trial* between hero and environment is symbolized in the fact that the first "reaction" in *The Castle* is the landlord's, who is "extremely surprised and confused (äusserst überrascht und verwirrt)"[7] by K.'s arrival. As Hillmann points out, the initial "shock" is experienced by the village, not the hero, thereby heightening the "reality" of the villagers in contrast to the "abstractness" of the hero: "This society then defends itself against this intrusion, just as elsewhere the hero defends himself against the threat to himself. The battlefronts are thus reversed."[8]

Kafka has embarked on the exceedingly difficult enterprise of making the reader feel that even the most "normal" reactions of the character through whose eyes the story is presented are somehow provisional, not quite alive, in effect *not* normal. The basis for this sense of alienation is established in the opening scene with Schwarzer, when the full flexibility of K.'s position as an outsider is displayed in the first and only direct confrontation with the Castle system. Understanding of K. is not furthered by thinking of his opening questions as lies or dissimulations. "What village is this I have wandered into? Is there a castle here? (In welches Dorf habe ich mich verirrt? Ist denn hier ein Schloss?)" The simple directness of these words represents extreme danger for the Castle: it is nighttime and K.'s fluid adoption of an outsider's identity makes it doubtful that he can be processed through the system's channels. He is, in effect, perilously close to making precisely the kind of apocalyptic nighttime request described so much later by Bürgel. It is significant that only in the first chapter is the figure at the apex of the Castle system, Count Westwest, frequently mentioned. In these first moments the abstract relationship of system and outsider is functioning in a way that does not later recur; indeed the response of Schwarzer to K.'s suggestion that he seek permission directly from the Count—"that's the only thing to be done (es wird nichts anderes übrigbleiben)"—is unusually revealing: "A permit from the Count in the middle of the night! (Jetzt um Mitternacht die Erlaubnis vom Herrn Grafen holen?)" The novel's subsequent development shows that such a thought is virtually unthinkable. But K. has thought it and Schwarzer can only react helplessly, bringing K.'s notion further into the realm of possibility by repeating his words. But K. cannot, because of his own incompleteness, know how close he is to immediate success, that the only figure the Castle will acknowledge directly is a total outsider; K. sees his quest for identity as a "campaign," a systematic struggle that will yield a result partaking of both insider and outsider.

The obvious parallels between K.'s "vocation" and Faust's "fulfilled moment" at the end of *Faust, Part Two* suggest that K. is a kind of Faust in reverse, a figure whose insistence on the strategies necessary to "construct" an identity draws him ever further from the almost-"fulfilled moment" at the novel's outset. Certainly the concept of a surveyor is, as Emrich says, "revolutionary" in the context of a system that is "totally organized" (Philippi). But ironically, K. presents his potentially radical vocation in a way that points away from its abstract significance and towards Sokel's view of it as merely a "calling," a profession that stands inside, not outside the system. "Enough of this comedy (Genug der Komödie)," says K.; and indeed he then proceeds to write the premature end of the only "play" he is ever able to initiate, dissolving the present moment in his talk of witnesses, of the next day, of going to sleep, yielding to the impulse to score points by, in effect, withdrawing from the attack: "That it was too late to present myself at the Castle I knew very well (Dass es jetzt zu spät war, im Schloss mich zu melden, wusste ich schon aus eigenem)." K.'s developing ambivalence is made explicit in his response to the presence of a telephone: "The particular instance surprised K., but on the whole he had really expected it."[9] As the emblem of the direct connection between himself and the Castle, the telephone merely makes concrete what K. himself had presumably felt on the bridge leading to the village. But as a "detail," a specific piece of equipment suggesting the interlocking dimensions of a system that excludes him, the telephone unsettles K. It is this world of "details" that is beginning to engulf him.

A technique used by Kafka to suggest the "provisional" quality in his protagonist is presentation from the outside. The paradoxical combination of the hero's perspective with such momentary withdrawals, found already in "Description of a Struggle," occurs frequently in the first chapter of *The Castle:* "K. did not change his position, did not even once turn round, seemed quite indifferent, and stared into space."[10] Compelled to view K. from the outside, the reader feels the strengths, as well as the exposure, of the outsider's posture. K.'s uninvolved assessment of Schwarzer's telephone manner and the Castle's workings shows his absorption in strategy to be formidable equipment for an outsider's identity. When the Castle, in momentary disarray, appears to solidify this identity by rejecting K., his response is cool to the point of abstraction: "To escape at least the first shock of their assault he crawled right underneath the blanket."[11] The Castle then recovers and puts itself into a position to convert K.'s strategic strength into weakness by confirming his appointment.

The next paragraph ("K. pricked up his ears . . . "), crucial to an interpretation of K., is full of ironies that suggest K.'s future dependence on the Castle at the moment of his most vivid declaration of independence. He is obviously right to see the appointment as a form of challenge, but because he cannot see the strength of his present position he fatally misstates the relationship. The Castle does indeed know "everything necessary about him (alles Nötige über ihn),"[12] namely, that he is a potential transformer of the system who must be fended off at all costs; its initiation of the struggle is thus hardly "with a smile" (*lächelnd*). K. perceives his appointment, correctly, as an effort by the Castle to coopt him and blunt his effort to achieve an identity through a direct relationship. But in this it turns out that the Castle has made a just (rather than an under-)estimation of him. For, like the man from the country in "Before the Law," K. has an inadequate idea of the meaning of freedom. He feels that freedom can be quantified, equated with intellectual lack of attachment, and then applied in larger or smaller doses as the relationship with the system seems to require. He does not see that one is either inside or outside the system, with no compromise possible. He fails to realize that, at the moment when he begins to reckon out the amount of freedom he can expect, he has in fact forfeited the only valid freedom, the freedom to relate to the Castle without any regard for its preferred modalities.

K. awakes the next morning determined to confront the Castle, making strategic use of the advantage he feels his appointment has given him. But gradually he becomes involved with village life, symbolized by the universal snow making everything more "definite" and more uniform. Given the intricacies of each individual snow crystal, there is no paradox in observing that the world of the village is both alive in every detail and undifferentiated in its overall patterning. On one level K. is one of the "forms" being gently covered by the Castle's snow: none of the four meetings with village inhabitants that take place during the remainder of this chapter is really initiated by K. He allows the landlord to satisfy an apparent urge to talk to him; while contemplating the Castle K. is "disturbed" (*gestört*) by the schoolteacher's presence; when the exhausted K. throws a snowball against the nearest window, the response—"the door opened immediately (Gleich öffnete sich die Tür)"—is as if he were expected; and Gerstäcker, who appears to know K.'s identity in advance, addresses him without prompting. However, it would be wrong to conclude, as too rigid an application of Walser's theory would seem to indicate, that the Castle is moving monolithically to counter K.'s self-assertions. In the villagers of the Castle we see fully developed what the narrator of "The Great Wall of China" has hinted at in his compatriots: fundamental oneness with the system and impenetrably sceptical individualism. "Total ambivalence," earlier the property of the hero-narrator, has been transferred to the environment, automatically invalidating K.'s efforts to establish his function, despite illusions of progress. For it is a feature of the reopened structure Kafka has developed here that the two basic currents—K.'s abstract relationship with the Castle and his human ties to the village—by no means coincide, and as a rule move in opposite directions. To take two obvious

examples: at the moment of K.'s greatest success, the winning of
Frieda, he experiences a sense of total alienation that rightly foreshadows how far this relationship will take him away from the Castle
in its abstract form; and, of course, the moment of total human defeat
and exhaustion is also the moment of proximity to success in Bürgel's
room. Between these extremes every encounter of K.'s entails the possibility of movement on both levels. And while I incline to agree with
Walser that "development" would contradict the basic conception of
K.'s "character," Kafka has infused the novel's structure with so strong
a feeling of the *possibility* of development that several critics, most
notably Gray and Emrich, detect an actual change in K. towards the
end of the existing text.

The encounter with the landlord begins the blurring of K.'s sense
of himself as outsider and raises the obsessive question of "power"
(*Macht*). But the tension of the scene arises from an explicit counter-
current: the landlord, within the framework of his limited personality,
tries to suggest to K. that he does not belong in the village, that his
only possible relationship is with the Castle itself. In K.'s responses
one can sense a division between the abstract need to "know" the realities of the situation and the ever-stronger urge to manipulate those
realities in the direction of the desired synthesis between the abstract
and the human. At the same time, although the scene is entirely coherent, with an "internal" reason offered for each of K.'s responses, an
experimental, theatrical impression predominates. The stage metaphor
seems to apply twice over: K. is consciously placing himself on stage,
seeking a tangible "relationship" with the landlord; but the scene itself
takes control of him, as well as being manipulated by him. This is most
evident in the foreshortened changes in his attitudes to the landlord.
At the outset we hear that K. "took pity on the man and asked him to
sit down for a while (erbarmte sich seiner und liess ihn für ein Weilchen
bei sich niedersetzen)"; after the first exchanges K.'s thought is, "His
confidence was not to be lightly won (Leicht war das Vertrauen dieses
Mannes nicht zu gewinnen)"; and at the end he is anxiously building
the illusion that there is a bond between them: "K. did not want to
force his confidence any farther, however, nor to scare away the smile
he had at last evoked."[13] Between the first two of these reactions K.
pursues two aims that turn out to be incompatible: leading the landlord
to reveal his attitude to the Castle and compelling him to identify himself with his function in the evident hope that K.'s own function will
become clearer. In fact the landlord does express himself quite clearly
about the Castle—its sphere is qualitatively different from his own—
but because this is not what K. wants to hear, he concentrates instead

on the relatively trivial matter of the landlord's function: "Was the landlord so willing, then, to give up prospective customers, and K. in particular, whom he so unconditionally transferred to the Castle?"[14] In his eagerness to pin down the landlord, K. "plays" with his own situation and in the process trivializes his own strengths. K.'s remark, "I want always to be free (Ich will immer frei sein),"[15] has been regarded as a statement of belief, but in its context it is quite the opposite, a reduction of the notion of freedom to the question of whether his spare time will be taken up by his job. K. has taken a step further towards the transformation of freedom into a relative value, a kind of adornment. The culmination of this process is the scene where K. waits for Klamm in the snow; far from bypassing the official channels with an outsider's directness, K. is here merely attempting, metaphorically, to gate-crash through the receptionist's office. His failure revives an understanding of his essentially abstract situation, in relation to which there is "nothing more senseless, nothing more hopeless, than *this* freedom (nichts Sinnloseres, nichts Verzweifelteres als *diese* Freiheit)" (my italics).[16]

The second part of the conversation with the landlord is dominated by the chamberlain's portrait, symbolically opening another dimension in the stage metaphor. Hitherto the dialogue has retained its "abstract" quality, in that K.'s focus on the fundamentals of the situation has not been diverted by any "props." The picture, however, inaugurates a steady movement towards the iconographic. The characters K. meets retain a well-defined individuality, but for K. they are beginning to merge with the scenery, withdrawing from him in a way that no longer surprises him (as the landlord's behavior surprises him). He is becoming a "surveyor" in a new sense: no longer the revolutionary standing outside, K. is caught up in the contemplation of the Castle as a systematic summation of all its details. His oscillating posture is predicated not only on the Castle's gestures of encouragement and rejection but also on his own ambivalence. While retaining his sense of the Castle as an abstract adversary, he eagerly explores the power relationships expounded by the villagers, accepting for this purpose the villagers' definitions of the limits of action, but ultimately always rejecting their advice. All this is foreshadowed by the chamberlain's portrait, not least in the fact that it does not portray the Count himself. K. accepts this symbolic change and lightly formulates the strategy of "using" his outsider's position to manipulate the power relationships. That such "play" represents a basic redirection of his quest for an identity is shown by his anxious study of the landlord's response.

Having accepted the Castle's framework, K. seeks from the villagers an impossible dual acknowledgment of both his correctness and his superiority. The initial success of the landlord's smile is of course ironic, a result of the latter's simple-mindedness, as K. half-realizes: "He was actually young, with that soft and almost beardless face of his (Er war wirklich ein Junge mit seinem weichen, fast bartlosen Gesicht)."

The specifics of the description of the Castle itself have been analyzed by many critics, notably Walter Sokel. My concern here is to situate this description in relation to K.'s other encounters during the first chapter. Essentially it marks a decisive broadening of the visual element introduced by the chamberlain's picture, drawing K. into itself with its strange concreteness while withdrawing into the flatness of a stage setting. K.'s first reaction to it is comparable to his early response to the existence of a telephone in the inn: "on the whole" (*im ganzen*) he had expected a castle that resembled a "little town" (*Städtchen*), embodying the functionality of human relationships in its outward aspect. But the "details" surprise him: not only is the Castle run down and lacking the "center" that a proper church tower would supply; the tower it does have is like a warning, suggestive of the total irrationality of the system he is approaching. For a moment K. seems to realize the irreconcilability of the castle's abstract and physical dimensions: "Again K. came to a stop, as if in standing still he had more power of judgment."[17] The tentative quality of all K.'s actions, expressed by the "as if" construction, does not obscure the significance of his simply standing still. In a fragment that seems related to *The Castle* in its imagery (the carriage is reminiscent of the carriage in which K. drinks Klamm's brandy), Kafka spells out the symbolic vanity of constant motion, even without the universally obstructive snow to drive the point home:

> If you perpetually run forwards, wading on in the lukewarm air, your hands thrust out like fins; if you glance fleetingly, in the dazed condition of incessant haste, at everything you pass, then one day you will let the carriage itself roll by unnoticed. But if you stand firm, spreading, through the strength of your gaze, roots both deep and wide—allowing nothing to budge you, even though these roots really do consist only in the strength of your purposeful gaze—then you will also see the unchangingly dark remoteness, from which nothing can come but, on that single occasion, the carriage; it rolls towards you,

grows in size, becomes, at the moment it reaches you, all-embracing and you sink down inside it like a child in the cushions of a coach driving through a storm at night.[18]

The paradox of K.'s position is that such cosmic equilibrium is both uniquely available to him, in his position as a de facto outsider, and virtually inaccessible because of his unusual susceptibility, being not yet defined, to the suggestive power of an environment that has already defined itself.

The conversation with the teacher is well calculated to destroy utterly K.'s residual interest in maintaining his equilibrium. The teacher is the opposite of the landlord. In his conversation with the landlord, K. had succumbed to the temptation to manipulate reality by eliciting a meaningless assent. The teacher, by contrast, responds unexpectedly to deliberately "conventional" questions by K., preventing him from even mentioning his function as surveyor, the potential "identity" with which he had toyed so expansively in the earlier conversation. Once again, and much more graphically, the teacher's words stress the difference between an abstract and a concrete relationship with the Castle. The Count's name is unmentionable in front of the children; yet "There is no difference between the peasantry and the Castle (Zwischen den Bauern und dem Schloss ist kein grosser Unterschied)." The villagers' lives are rooted in the organization of the Castle, but life inside the system implies total acceptance of the hierarchy, thereby making the man at the top unimaginably remote. K., as an outsider, is bound to "dislike" the system. His proper relationship is with the Count directly; hence no existence is conceivable for him in the village. But K. cannot take this in; mishearing the teacher's emphasis, he requests a meeting to discuss that which cannot be discussed in front of the children. As in the conversation with the landlord, the episode concludes with K.'s insistence, this time without any response comparable to a smile, on the initiation of a "relationship."

The teacher's uncompromising directness in suggesting what K. does not want to hear disorients K. completely: "disconcerted" (*zerstreut*), no longer clear as to his purpose, he resumes the trudge towards the Castle in a mood ready, even anxious, for the kind of defeat that will involve the lucidity of "destruction" rather than the incipient "crumbling" of his present position. The language evokes K.'s growing passivity: "at last he tore himself away from the obsession of the street and escaped into a small side-lane."[19] The stage is thus literally set for the withdrawal of the Castle world into the flatness of a backdrop, withholding from the principal actor the longed-for clarity of defeat. The first words of the scene in Lasemann's house, phrased like stage directions, express this withdrawal: "A large kitchen, dimly lit. Anyone coming in from outside could make out nothing at first."[20] Hints that this functioning domestic world, with all the necessary components of life, is really a kind of genre painting are conveyed through the stylized language: "Several children were playing around her . . . . The woman at the washtub, young, plump, and fair, sang in a low voice as she worked."[21] This interior scene corresponds functionally to the exterior of the Castle K. has already observed. It too has a centerpiece that gives an unsettling effect to the scene as a whole. The oddly irrational Castle tower, with its suggestion of excess life, has its counterpart in the lifeless "girl from the Castle (Mädchen aus dem Schloss)," so noticeable amid all the vitality. The Castle world expresses itself in polarities which can appear rational only to those within the system: life and lifelessness, pedantry and haste, hierarchy and informality, hope and resignation.

Having literally succumbed, in sleep, to the illusion of oneness with the scene before him, K. is fully prepared, upon awakening, for the experience of rejection. Such a sequence of events—the witnessing of something exceptional followed by eviction as an interloper—would constitute precisely the kind of negative acknowledgment of his identity that he craves: when told he must leave, K. "was pleased by the man's frankness (freute sich über die offenen Worte)." But K. cannot extract any recognition of his individuality. His role as surveyor does not entitle him to any special "hospitality" (*Gastfreundlichkeit*), but neither is he being expelled for any personal reasons—"we . . . stick to our tradition (wir . . . halten uns an die Regel)." The impersonality of the procedure is underlined by the fact that two men address him, using the plural form, in contrast to earlier dialogues; apart from the special significance critics have discerned in Kafka's groupings of two figures, the manner of the two men suggests stiffness, ritual, as if the vitality they had displayed as part of the "scene" were suddenly drained away. In ironic contrast is the response of the statuesque lady to K.'s attempt to confirm and make specific his sense of an exceptional experience. Her words—"a girl from the Castle"—and their accompanying tone of contempt are indeed clear, but again in a way that dissolves K.'s expectations. She is not so "exceptional," just a girl without hieratic significance; her connection with the Castle is an unremarkable part of her life, a social attribute. Thus the apparent order of the "backdrop" dissolves: the "dead" centerpiece reenters a life of relative banality (she reappears later in the novel, without any aura apart from sickliness) while the men who had surrounded it with vitality become pedantic appliers of "rules." Once again K. tries to establish a "relationship" with the men who have thrown him out, this time with unambiguous lack of success; and with theatrical suddenness he is thrust back into isolation. Although physical confirmation is now given to the message of the earlier conversations—that K. should accept that he is by definition an outsider—K.'s only reaction is to insist on the "shape" of his experiences; the sequence of events has been "by design" (*absichtlich*), not "by accident" (*zufällig*), and thus the protagonist himself strives to endow the open-ended situation with the dramatic meaning of a closed structure.

In the chapter's final encounter, Gerstäcker clarifies once again the villagers' view of K.: he "belongs" to the Castle in a direct relationship that excludes the villagers by definition. And again K. prefers not to hear the meaning behind Gerstäcker's refusal to drive him to the Castle, treating it as a matter of whim, a personal rejection to be answered with the correct strategy, here that of "reculer pour mieux sauter": "Oh, well, take me to the inn (Dann fahrt mich also zum Wirtshaus)." During the journey the Castle itself comments on the situation with the mockingly ambivalent sound of bells. It is impossible, indeed undesirable, to reduce this gesture to a single meaning. The Castle bell is a kind of will-o'-the-wisp, preventing K. from reaching an acceptance of his exclusion that alone could produce clarity, by holding out possibilities of "fulfillment." At the same time the single tone of the Castle bell, contrasting with the "tinkle" (*Geklingel*) of the village, suggests the fundamental dualism of the situation and the "single" opportunity that K. has, as opposed to the multiple approaches he is trying to develop. Then again, the continuity between Castle and village bells tends to confirm the "inside" course on which K. is engaged. Such unfathomable enigmas constitute the Castle's prime defense against the threat it fears, the undiverted gaze of a determined outsider.

The scene with Gerstäcker is laid out in detailed contrast to K.'s experience in Lasemann's house. There K. had entertained the illusion of harmony with a static picture of the Castle world; here he is offered the momentary illusion of mobility, a journey that is merely the cancellation of his own earlier movements. The interior scene had evoked the lure of relationships, of meanings that bind individuals together; Gerstäcker, by contrast, is utterly without resonance, tonelessly repeating what K. says to him, pointing in no direction except back towards K. himself. Most important of all, the Lasemann scene had ended with finality, with K.'s unambiguous exclusion. In the wholly unpromising figure of Gerstäcker, however, Kafka has found a medium to express the essence of the reopened structure. The dismal quality of his appearance and manner evoke an unexpected reaction in K.— sympathy. This sympathy is in no sense a central feature of K.'s character, but its appearance underlines the embryonic conception of that character. Accustomed to the schematic Josef K., the reader is frequently startled by the "conventional" responses of K. in *The Castle*. These responses are fragments of an identity that K. is seeking to integrate, but the novel's structure implies that the more such fragments emerge in the hero's relationships with the villagers, the more remote are his chances of achieving the only functional identity available to him, that of the outsider. Because K. himself has chosen the pattern of his existence, without any direct intervention by the Castle after his initial appointment, the novel's episodes freely counterpoint K.'s reductionist tendencies with a proliferation of self-sufficient individualities. The two basic elements in the reopened structure are the formulaic and the unexpected, fictional expressions of the functional and the arbitrary.

If this interpretation seems more tendentious than earlier discussions, it is because the complex ground plan of *The Castle* demands such an approach. Thus, although the basic contrast between abstract and concrete links to the Castle is not spelled out specifically until the scene in Bürgel's room, the frequency of the hints pointing in this direction throughout the chapter suggests that the reader is already expected to "judge" K.'s performance in terms of the play as a whole, despite its inaccessibility. K.'s calculating responses to the villagers tend to disguise the fact that they are all telling him the same thing about himself. More seriously, it could be objected that my conception of K. is artificial, even meaningless: how can one speak of an "unformed" character who appears to possess a full array of faculties? What does it mean to equate the posture of an outsider with a functional identity? Such questions are inherent in the attempt to root "character" in the polarities of the functional and the arbitrary and there are some striking statements by Kafka that clarify the paradoxical situation to which he is here giving fictional expression. Throughout Kafka's life he referred to himself, in letters and diary entries, as "unborn"; that he meant by this not emptiness but, on the contrary, an unhealthily teeming existence below the surface of "reality" is evoked in a vivid phrase in a letter of October 1917 to Max Brod: "I seem to myself to be unborn; myself something dark, I lunge in the darkness."[22]

In a diary entry of 24 January 1922, at the beginning, that is, of
what Pasley and Wagenbach consider to be the period of intensive
work on *The Castle*, Kafka formulated this feeling more abstractly and
followed it with a paragraph suggesting the close proximity of the idea
of "birth" to that of self-recognition, acceptance of what one already is:

> Hesitation before birth. If there is a transmigration of souls,
> then I am not yet on the bottom rung. My life is a hesitation
> before birth.
>   Steadfastness. I don't want to pursue any particular course
> of development. I want to change my place in the world en-
> tirely, which actually means that I want to go to another planet;
> it would be enough if I could exist alongside myself, it would
> even be enough if I could consider the spot on which I stand as
> some other spot.[23]

K.'s position is that of an outsider; so long as he understands by this
a state of exclusion, alterable through "development," from a world
that should be joined, his whole existence is merely a "hesitation." The
only answer, which he is incapable of perceiving, is radical acceptance
of the outsider's status: then the whole system confronting him would
become powerless before the directness of his gaze. *The Castle* is the
articulation of a continuous "hesitation," an attempt to avoid, or rather
circumvent, the moment of "birth." To this end Kafka has to maintain
a persisting dual awareness in the reader: the villagers must be "alive,"
embodiments of a genuine community, and also members of an abstract system who understand K.'s position better than he does. And
K., as the consciousness through which events are filtered, is felt as a
single character; yet his words and actions suggest a fragmented identity, unfocused aims masked by an obsession with strategic details.
That Kafka instinctively used the theatrical metaphor to express such
a dualism is made clear in the diary entry in which there also appears
the first direct reference to *The Castle* (29 January 1922):

> . . . I am too far away, am banished, have—since I am human
> after all and my roots want nourishment—my proxies "down"
> (or up) there too, sorry, unsatisfactory comedians who can
> satisfy me (though indeed they don't satisfy me at all and it
> is for this reason that I am so forsaken) only because I get my
> principal nourishment from other roots in other climes, these
> roots too are sorry ones, but nevertheless better able to sustain
> life.[24]

There is no question of a crass identification of K. with Kafka himself: Kafka is aware of his own "otherness" whereas K. is not. Kafka's "proxies" perform their minimal functions and withdraw; K.'s tentative, earnestly acted personae strive vainly to transform both themselves and the stage on which they are playing into a single, continuous reality.

10 Historical Structure: "Josefine the Singer, or the Mouse Folk"

The open-ended structure of *The Castle* is predicated on the theorem that the deeper K.'s involvement with the essentially alien lives of the villagers, the further he moves from an understanding of his own situation, so that when confronted with his unique opportunity he does not recognize it. Clearly Kafka was tempted to imagine a situation in which this theorem did not apply, in which the outsider would be able to recognize his abstract relationship to society and, as it were, say the words that K. can never say. Kafka's last volume of stories is concerned primarily with exploring the interaction between society and outsiders who have accepted their situation as one uniting function with identity. In "Josefine the Singer,"[1] especially, Kafka presents a relationship analogous to that between K. and the Castle in that it is based on power: "Josefine asserts herself, a mere nothing in voice, a mere nothing in execution, she asserts herself and gets across to us."[2] This sentence summarizes the key qualities that differentiate Josefine from K.: she has placed herself outside all traditional avenues to power, recognizing that by being much less than a singer she can become much more than one, creating a "way" where none had existed. In a quite specific sense she fulfills Kafka's dictum: "There is a goal, but no way; what we call a way is hesitation."[3] Josefine has achieved the dominance that awaits the outsider who can accept his own isolation: she compels society to organize itself in relation to her, gladly following her whims even at the risk of death. The fact that an "opposition" to her exists merely confirms her hold over society: as the narrator makes clear, the opposition entertains intellectual doubts about her qualities but submits like everyone else when she asserts herself.

The difficulty with such a character is that it is basically hypothetical, unrealizable even within the relatively wide range of responses allowed to K. in *The Castle*; the self-knowledge necessary to achieve Josefine's position is something Kafka could only formulate theoretically. In the figure of the hunger-artist he presses human psychology to the edge of mysticism, and even in his prime the hunger-artist is only a sideshow, never a functionally important element in society. So Kafka has distanced the reader from Josefine in three fundamental respects: her preeminence is "given"—the question of how it was attained is left unasked; she is a mouse, so that the reader is discouraged from inquiring too closely into the actual mechanism of her dominance; and by the device of the skeptical narrator Kafka ensures that the questions that might trouble the reader are all asked before they occur to him. This ingenious use of a narrator who is allowed some individual traits without ever becoming an "individual" brings Josefine alive while restricting her to her functional, public persona: the narrator notices enough that is individual about both her and her audience to prevent the story from becoming either an eccentric's tale (like "A Hunger-Artist") or a political study.

According to Brod, Kafka attached some importance to the "or" (*oder*) in his title: it suggests that he has created a unique dual history, the history of an individual who would not "be" without the society that supports her—and of a society that does not write history and in its perpetual flux welcomes the moments of static ritual Josefine imposes on it. The use of "or" rather than "and" in the title emphasizes the basic antagonism between the two elements in the history. The mice submit to Josefine the outsider precisely because she is an outsider and must always remain one. Kafka's "historical structure" is a unique blend of the reductive, static mode of society, analytic prose, with the directional, fluid mode of individual identity, the drama. "Josefine, the Singer" constitutes an extreme example of Kafka's method of combining contradictory principles, defined by Ulrich Fülleborn as "perspectivist" (*perspektivisch*) and "parabolic" (*parabolisch*).[4] It is extreme because, whereas in the works of Kafka narrated from the protagonist's perspective the parabolic principle emerges gradually from the rhythm of failure, here the creation and destruction of a myth proceed simultaneously. Josefine's mythopeic claims are ultimately negated by her dependence on a society that would reject her if it could; but the narrator's efforts to extract a permanent "meaning" from the situation are equally frustrated by the heroine's sheer quirkiness, by what to him appears as suicidal vanity. With all the trappings and gestures of drama at his disposal, the narrator nevertheless finds his subject "crumbling" as he seeks to reduce it to socially usable prose. The confrontation between K. and the Castle is thus reenacted, on an elemental level and with the perspective reversed.

The resulting "historical structure" unites three strands in Kafka's work on which this study has focused: the antithetical perception of reality, as originally embodied in the image of "tree trunks in the snow"; the use of theatrical metaphors to convey the human quest for identity; and the device of function, widening the implications of an individual life. Two concurrent structures can be observed in the story, belying the formally static presentation. On the analytic level, indeed, the narrator struggles to maintain a stasis, attempting to encompass all the elements in the situation by a systematic use of antithesis. At the outset the method seems to work, as the narrator dismantles all Josefine's claims to being exceptional but is able to discern the special qualities of her performance in its exaggerated ordinariness. Anticipating the Campbell soup can, Josefine's "art" is merely ordinary life detached from its context and turned into an object of contemplation by an act of mutual agreement between performer and public. The performance itself synthesizes the contradictions:

> Josefine does not want mere admiration, she wants to be admired exactly in the way she prescribes, mere admiration leaves her cold. And when you take a seat before her, you understand her; opposition is possible only at a distance, when you sit before her, you know: this piping of hers is no piping.[5]

The key sentence here is "And when you take a seat before her, you understand her," a sentence that papers over, as it were, all the potential cracks in the surface. "And" is truly a connective, uniting Josefine's radical individualism with the people's response, but it is put in question by "understand," which implies only that the people see why Josefine makes her demands, not that they accept them. And the whole relationship is qualified by the repeated "when you sit before her": Josefine is an individual seeking acknowledgment of her preeminence as such—but what she receives is total submission for the duration of her performance, which amounts to no acknowledgment at all, but rather the exploitation of her for communal purposes.

All the sources of tension are thus implied by the narrator even while he is expounding the situation as stable. The narrator's aspiration is essentially linguistic, to become the "historian" of a people without history by organizing his perceptions around a specific phenomenon; and thus the disintegration of his theme is also linguistic, as the mystical and worldly components of the subject fall into ever greater discord and the ever more ambitious antitheses cease to function as modes of reintegration. The basic movement of the story is from deceptive clarity through flux to total paradox, as can be seen from the narrator's efforts to formulate both his own role and that of Josefine at different stages of the exposition. At the outset "Our singer is called Josefine": individual and function are at one. And the narrator feels able to make quite precise statements implying that his people is sufficiently aware of its own existence in time to possess legends and traditions:

> Although we are unmusical we have a tradition of singing; in the old days our people did sing; this is mentioned in legends and some songs have actually survived, which, it is true, no one can now sing.[6]

In the middle of the story nothing is clear. We are told of Josefine's "never quite defined position (niemals ganz geklärten Stellung)"; and the historian still exists as a concept, even as an infrequent reality: " . . . although at the cost of sacrifices which make historians—generally speaking we ignore historical research entirely—quite horror-struck."[7] Having defined both Josefine and, by implication, himself in terms of function, the narrator is driven by the logic of his exposition to undermine these functions; but a loss of function would mean a loss of existence, a cancellation of the whole structure erected upon the counterpoint of observer and observed.

This is in effect what happens at the end, when Josefine's disappearance impels the narrator to attempt to salvage his own structure by paradoxically reversing the roles of Josefine and the people. Since the question, "How can our gatherings take place in utter silence? (Wie werden die Versammlungen in völliger Stummheit möglich sein?)," is essentially unanswerable, the narrator puts forward the idea that Josefine is no longer necessary, indeed never was necessary, to the people's self-awareness. In other words the people "include" Josefine's power within themselves. Before the reader can interject that such an idea contradicts the earlier description of Josefine as the only organizing principle of a people in perpetual fearful motion, the narrator hurries on to the second half of his paradox: Josefine has become "the people," or rather, has entered the pantheon of heroes by which a people defines itself. Unfortunately, not only does the people lack the concept of individuation that makes a "hero" possible (there is a "numberless throng" of heroes), the absence of history, which is now seen as total, means that the whole story of Josefine is without legitimate meaning. Thus Josefine exists "in heightened redemption (in gesteigerter Erlö-sung),"[8] a phrase amounting to a symmetrical abolition of her initial definition as "singer." Emrich, who terms this story Kafka's "swan song," thereby falling into the fallacy of regarding the last thing he wrote as the last thing he meant to write, discerns positive meaning in the words *gesteigerte Erlösung*.[9] To my mind, they constitute a stroke of extreme literary irony, reminiscent of K.'s use of the term "freedom" in his conversation with the landlord. "Redemption," like freedom, is by definition unquantifiable, a word evoking that unity between self and world for which all Kafka's heroes vainly strive. By combining it with the meaningless "heightened," and by using it so blatantly to offset the bleak emptiness of his story's end, the narrator devalues his entire attempt to give structure and "history" to his society through the discriminations of language. As the perspective here is not Josefine's but the narrator's own, the phrase turns inward onto the literary enterprise itself: since he has dissolved the basis of his own narrative, this linguistic expression of dissolution stands for the only level on which he and his heroine exist, the level of words, words emptied of the concrete connectedness that initially justified them.

The factor that has brought about this transformation of functional clarity into impossible paradox is the arbitrary restlessness of both sides, the accelerating oscillation between individual and collective that is held in precarious balance by the mutually agreed self-limitation of the "performance." The disruption of this balance, for both Josefine and her would-be historian, begins openly with the paragraph "Yet there is something else behind it . . . (Nun spricht aber doch noch anderes mit herein . . .)." Josefine's assertion that it is she who protects the people and not vice versa represents the kind of uncompromising individualism that the narrator cannot absorb by his antitheses. Gradually these antitheses move beyond the limits of common sense which had seemed to contain them comfortably at the start. Josefine's arrogance is countered by the sophistry that, as the people are unmusical, the fact that they listen to her is "proof that she is no singer (ein Beweis gegen ihren Gesang)." This negative swing of the pendulum is offset by the tying of Josefine's status to the "childishness" (*Kindlichkeit*) of the people. When a redefinition of her music in exclusively social terms again seems inadequate to the phenomenon that is Josefine, the narrator elevates his description to a quasi-mystical level: "Something of our poor brief childhood is in it, something of lost happiness that can never be found again."[10] Pulling himself up short, the narrator reminds himself of the exaggerated claims Josefine has made for herself: "But from that point it is a long, long way to Josefine's claim that she gives us new strength and so on and so forth."[11] A relationship to which only the intimate terminology of the family had seemed appropriate is finally stated in terms of naked power: " . . . perhaps as individuals the people may surrender too easily to Josefine, but as a whole they surrender unconditionally to no one, and not to her either."[12]

Josefine's individualistic demands are formally responsible for this fundamental closing of the ranks against her. But, as the narrator sees it, the bond between singer and people is so deep-rooted that he feels impelled to apply his dialectic even to this seemingly basic fact: has not the people, in its self-destructive "wisdom," so structured the situation that Josefine would necessarily be impelled to make unacceptable demands?

> Suppose that instead of the people one had an individual to deal with: one might imagine that this man . . . had sacrificed more than was needful merely to hasten the process, merely to spoil Josefine and encourage her to ask for more and more until she did indeed reach the limit with this last petition of hers; and that he then cut her off with a final refusal which was curt because long held in reserve. Now, this is certainly not how the matter stands.[13]

Such speculations cannot ultimately be entertained. In the final confrontation, the narrator is driven back to the side of his own people, upholding the legitimacy of their responses. But because his story, indeed his very perception of reality, is predicated on the functional relationship between Josefine and the people, his last pages are devoted entirely to the vivid detailing of her behavior. Bringing her to the center of the stage represents both the disintegration of a structure built on balance and rationality and an effort to recover the tangible material of his story before its final disappearance.

The breakdown of the narrator's aspirations towards stasis brought about by Josefine's self-assertion can, however, be seen as merely a counterpoint to a theme that gradually becomes explicit: the emergence of a drama with individual contours from the very process of narration. Josefine's stubborn finale is, in the original context of "tree trunks in the snow," the culminating manifestation of the winter's snow before its disappearance from the world it has functionally dominated for so long, into the realm of memory and illusion. Even more compellingly, these scenes represent the final act of a drama that the reader has barely been aware of until it is almost over. Kafka has often employed the theatrical analogy to illustrate the efforts of his heroes to impose their own fictions on the reality that confronts them. Here the image is applied in reverse: Josefine is explicitly on stage, and moreover a stage at several removes from the reader, mediated by a narrator who both calls the performance into question and seeks to integrate it into his own schema. But Josefine refuses to accept a performer's limitations and, by her sisyphean attempt to replace the audience's instinctual flux with a social order based solely on her definition of art, forces her way out into the unmediated world of the reader's own reality.

Josefine's "drama" can be divided into three "acts." At the beginning she is content to be defined in terms of her social function. That this involves deliberate restraints on her individuality is made clear by her "smile so sarcastic and arrogant (freches, hochmütiges Lächeln)" when it is suggested that her "singing" is identical with that of the audience. At this point decorum visibly dictates her responses: "she was at once aware of it herself, by the way, with her extreme sensibility, and controlled herself."[14] Simply because art cannot exist without an audience, she accepts the fact that her performance has become a ritual, that variation and sublety will go unnoticed: "she has long learned not to expect real understanding, as she conceives it (auf wirkliches Verständnis, wie sie es meint, hat sie längst verzichten gelernt)." The tensions inherent in this situation emerge into the open in the second "act," which is announced by the paragraph beginning "And if small events do her such service, how much more do great ones (Wenn ihr aber nun das Kleine so dient, wie erst das Grosse)." This phase could be termed the high Renaissance of Josefine's art, in contrast to the quasi-anonymous Gothic synthesis of her beginnings and the mannerist decadence of the conclusion. In this central section Josefine turns her dependence on an audience into something positive by identifying her art with periods of stress and crisis in the life of the people. Politics and art feed each other: if her audience cannot be brought to "understand" what it hears, at least it can be compelled, by making sacrifices in order to be present at her concerts, to acknowledge the importance of Josefine's art. By incorporating the emotional stress of a dangerous situation into her performance, Josefine transforms her singing into "a message from the whole people (eine Botschaft des Volkes)": her individual status grows in proportion to her self-identification with the upheavals experienced by her audience.

But this situation contains the seeds of its own disruption even more decisively than the imposed restraints of the first act. For the more Josefine extracts virtually unassailable prestige from the synthesis of art and politics, the more troublesome to her enhanced individuality becomes the fact that her art remains inseparable from a performance in time, ceasing to exist at the end of each performance; because "understanding" is unattainable, the only possibility of stability lies in a public acknowledgment that she is what she says she is and what every performance proves her to be. Thus the stage is set for the third "act" that opens with the paragraph "For a long time back, perhaps since the very beginning of her artistic career, Josefine has been fighting."[15] The words point to the dynamics of the story: the narrator always speaks in the present tense, as if he were describing a single situation rather than a sequence of events—yet only now does he unveil a fact that has supposedly existed for a long time. In other words, the narrator, as he shapes events sequentially in order to make a "narrative" possible, enacts a performance analogous to the performances he is trying to evoke. Josefine's life resists the logical framework of a phenomenon that is "analyzed" and imposes its own dramatic shape on the story, achieving individuality through the narrative of an "opponent" seeking to demonstrate the futility of such ambitions.

There are two ways of viewing the final act of Josefine's drama, for both of which the narrator offers explicit support. Seen from one angle her story has tragic dimensions: so absorbed has she become in the importance of her art that its compromised state—confinement to performances before an uncomprehending audience—has become intolerable to her. She is driven to demand a unique status not because she needs it, but because her art needs it:

> If she makes demands it is not because of outward circumstances but because of an inner logic. She reaches for the highest garland not because it is momentarily hanging a little lower but because it is the highest; if she had any say in the matter she would have it still higher.[16]

With this view the final events have a tragic inevitability: incapable of compromising her art to attract attention, Josefine cuts, then restores the "coloratura" passages, then resorts to prima donna-like mannerisms to sway her audience: "And so we get a theatrical performance as well as a concert (Wir haben nun ausser dem Konzert auch ein Schauspiel)." The dualistic detachment of the narrator's tone implies that the paradoxical "reality" of the performance has been tainted by fictions that only thrust singer and audience further apart. Realizing that her art has, after all, been irrevocably compromised, Josefine takes the only way out, preserving her art through the elimination of her person.

Curiously, this elevated logical explanation of Josefine's disappearance does not satisfy the narrator, although he has supplied the impetus for it. Suddenly her "inner logic" has become calculation, or rather miscalculation; but even as the narrator draws back from her he provides hints that bring Josefine even closer to the reader, pushing aside the veil of "art" in which she has been clothed:

> Curious, how mistaken she is in her calculations, the clever creature, so mistaken that one might fancy she has made no calculations at all but is only being driven on by her destiny, which in our world cannot be anything but a sad one. Of her own accord she abandons her singing, of her own accord she destroys the power she has gained over people's hearts. How could she ever have gained that power, since she knows so little about these hearts of ours?[17]

The answer to this last rhetorical question is contained within it: Josefine gained her position of power because she had adopted the role of outsider and, by definition, did not "know" the people she dominated. If she did know them in any nonfunctional sense she would not have been able to sustain the tensions of a direct relationship with the people, as opposed to individuals. From this perspective, Josefine's demands arose out of her growing involvement with public events in the central part of the story: her art had never been more than a confidence trick, a hypnotic illusion that sustained her power. Once this power seemed limitless, causing people to risk their lives to hear her, she succumbed to the illusion that it really was limitless; the strains of an outsider's life no longer seemed worth bearing and she moved to attain that "continuous reality" which hovers before K., in *The Castle*, as a chimera that yet seems readily attainable. But as Josefine desires to reenter society while retaining the unique powers of the outsider, her ambition amounts to self-destructive hubris. A royal position, to which she aspires, represents a synthesis between unquestioned dominance and the continuity of an insider's existence; that is why one can only be born to such a position. Yet the pursuit of the elusive combination of power and legitimacy has been the subject of so many dramatic conceptions that the fascination of Josefine is even enhanced by a view of her that would discount her devotion to "art."

In *The Castle* Kafka freed his structure from the novel's traditional dependence on "motivation" by using the perspective of a fragmented, incomplete hero; here he has in effect written a drama with two alternative endings, and at the same time enclosed his heroine in such a complexity of public perspectives that speculation about her motives becomes absorbed into her persona as an artist whose ultimate "performance" is the story built around her.

Through the interlocking dimensions of the historical structure Josefine has "achieved" what Karl Rossmann, with his unmediated relationship to events, never could: the fusion of autonomy and anonymity in a momentarily balanced world. The unique instability of Josefine's personal theater, resisting both her own "remedial" efforts and the narrator's attempts at codification, has become a source of permanence, of success rooted in a multiplicity of failures. As in the parallel historical structure, "A Little Woman" (1923), the fusion of Kafka's two "elements" ("closed," formalized reiteration on the one hand, "openness" of unlimited contingency on the other) is realized through a dramatization of the narrative act together with a drenching of the story's texture in the original terror of the Kafka-bachelor, time passing.

11   The Making of Kafka's Heroes

The irreducible element of Kafka's world is the voice: every phrase has a speaker. After centuries of mimesis the reader's response is automatically synthetic: he fleshes out the written words with his own experience in order to transform the speaker into a "character," a self-sufficient image spanning the separate worlds of author and reader. At the same time Kafka was well aware that the culmination of the mimetic tradition in naturalism had rendered the articulation of an exclusively fictional world impossible. Accustomed to an ever-decreasing gap between fiction and "reality," the reader of Kafka's time had developed an analytic sense, an insistence on verisimilitude that continually questioned the synthesizing process whereby fictional characters had come into being. Kafka's response was to incorporate both reactions of the reader, the synthetic and the analytic, the constructive and the destructive, into an entirely new approach to the notion of character. Virtually all of his stories are focused on a single hero: yet nothing is harder than to evolve an image of the "character" of a Kafka hero, even though he is usually placed very close to the reader's perspective, makes constant appeals to common sense, and seemingly has nothing to hide.

In "Description of a Struggle" the analytic impulse is allowed full play; both naturalistic conventions and Hoffmannesque dream worlds are invoked, played off against each other, and dissolved. Kafka demonstrates the uselessness of insisting on any one level of reality by creating a perpetuum mobile of illusion. But the unsettling variety of voices, even in the second version which retains a nominally continuous narrator, attenuates the story's interest, propelling each new "feeling," even explicit anguish, into the realm of the grotesque. The assault on the conventions of the past points only to the need for a new modality of understanding between author and reader. Kafka's eventual response, in "The Stoker," is to confront his literary situation; in Karl Rossmann's struggle to remake the world in the image of order, Kafka articulated the modern storyteller's estrangement from the narrative act and his need to reconstitute some kind of continuous signification. An unusually aesthetic theme is embedded in an unusually concrete texture. But the uncontaminated gaze of Karl Rossmann, the limits placed on his perspective by his lack of self-interest, make this carefully constructed world almost as hard for the reader to enter as the coruscations of "Description of a Struggle."

The experience of the theater enabled Kafka to achieve an unimpeded style of his own. The incorporation into mimetic conventions of theatrical techniques, specifically the actor's method of "presenting" the role he is playing, allowed the reintegration of the synthetic and analytic elements in the fictional voice. Quite simply, Kafka lets the heroes of "The Judgment" and "The Metamorphosis" present both themselves and their world. Mimetic conventions are upheld in a vacuum, they compel the reader to question rather than to accept both scenery and players; the hero's world can no longer be meaningfully separated from the hero's version of it. Not that the hero controls it, or even perceives it "correctly"; on the contrary, a basic discrepancy in the hero's view of himself is felt by the reader from the outset. But the hero has to be his own judge and jury; aware that the hero is wrong, the reader cannot say what is right. Thus the story presented by Georg Bendemann becomes "a whole building whose foundation walls have been torn up out of the earth with a force which today is still close to madness." The "wholeness" of the worlds of "The Judgment" and "The Metamorphosis" makes them unique among Kafka's works. The destruction of Georg Bendemann and of Gregor Samsa is symmetrically balanced against their self-constructions, industrious cartographies of the mind which only the mind can refute. Because he accepts the father's refutation, Georg ceases to exist; but Gregor's unwavering attachment to his own view of himself gains him a dignity untouched by death in disgusting circumstances.

The innovative elements that are held in balance by the familial framework of these stories become intensified to the point of generating the closed structure of *The Trial*. The autonomy of the hero is now absolute; the shadowy figures of the Court, however hostile, seem like outgrowths of his own persona. At the same time the blatant discrepancy in Josef K.'s responses to a seemingly self-created world becomes a constant, even predictable, element in his "character." Use of the theatrical analogy has enabled Kafka to formulate the stable basis essential to a longer work of fiction. The reader may never "know" Josef K., but he comes to know extremely well the role Josef K. has resolved on playing, the role of militant innocent. The discrepancy between that role and the response appropriate to the situation leads to the image of a hero both elusive and consistent, functioning at several levels without ever laying explicit claim to "depth." In counterpoint with Josef K. is the circumscribed, monochromatic figure of the explorer in "In the Penal Colony." If Josef K. knows himself to be at the center of events and adopts a role blending self-justification with a formula of escape, the explorer feels comfortably detached, without any sense of being called on to perform. The parablelike fusion of psychology and symbol in the mutual destruction of explorer and officer suggests the paradoxical freedom opened up by the closed structure: the freedom to display the dispassionate dissolution of apparent normality as well as the flooding of the public realm by obsessive self-images.

This structural freedom is fully utilized by Kafka in his last phase. Without sacrificing the controlling perspective of the hero, he reintegrates the hero's existence with an arbitrary universe by means of the a priori definition of "character" in terms of a willed function. In no sense is Kafka proceeding "beyond" the individual to confront "social" questions. On the contrary, by reestablishing a reality that insists on its tangible presence as the hero's audience, antagonist, and stage in one, Kafka has broadened the range of possibilities for evoking the fragmented, self-contradictory nature of the human mind. In *The Trial* the stable element that makes a long narrative possible is provided, not by the elusive Court, but by the self-defining role Josef K. has chosen to enact. The reader is in a claustrophobic mental theater, without hope of alternative perspectives. *The Castle*, however, juxtaposes an experimental hero with a rigid hierarchy, an unchanging physical stage which yet seems as provisional, as vulnerable, as the hero himself. The theatrical metaphor has shifted from the actor to the stage as a whole; the Castle functions like a populated stage without a principal actor, a world of self-contained people who are yet aware of the need for an act of definition such as only the outsider K. can provide. While the Castle disguises through bustling activity its readiness for an end, K. searches restlessly for a beginning; new facets of his "character" are constantly becoming prominent, while the possibility of synthesis, the mutual definition of self and society, continually recedes. Instead of being "destroyed," the hero "crumbles."

The simultaneous movement towards outward self-definition and inward fragmentation is characteristic of all Kafka's late stories. Josefine's achieved relationship with society dissolves even as its history is being told; the hunger-artist fulfills a lifetime ambition of indefinite fasting only to return to the corrosive initial lie; even the animal in "The Burrow," whose world is wholly self-created, cannot achieve the "continuous reality" which the insistent voices of Kafka's fiction both seek and undermine, with a Utopian skepticism masked as rationality. Kafka's later heroes are as tentative and fragile as the narrator of "Description of a Struggle"; their consistency of purpose and variety of strategies leave them as alien from the continuity they seek as a heavy snowfall from the tree trunk it envelops.

Whether the Kafka-hero tries to incorporate the world into his mental theater, to become the spectator of his own drama, or to reenter the world through the alignment of private role with public function, the result is the same: the "audience" he has sought to manipulate insists that he remain on stage perpetually. The metamorphosis of the theater, so indefatigably imagined, never takes place.

Notes

The original German has only been included when the nuances of textual analysis seem to require it. All references are to the standard German editions of Kafka's works, as designated by the following abbreviations. Full bibliographical information may be found in the list of Sources Consulted.

A	*Amerika*
B	*Beschreibung eines Kampfes*
Br	*Briefe 1902–1924*
BZF	*Beschreibung eines Kampfes: Die zwei Fassungen*
E	*Erzählungen*
H	*Hochzeitsvorbereitungen auf dem Lande und andere Prosa aus dem Nachlass*
P	*Der Prozess*
S	*Das Schloss*
T	*Tagebücher*

Standard translated edition:

D1	*Diaries, 1910–1913*
D2	*Diaries, 1914–1923*

Abbreviations for titles of journals:

DVLG	*Deutsche Vierteljahrschrift für Literaturwissenschaft und Geistesgeschichte*
GQ	*German Quarterly*
NDH	*Neue Deutsche Hefte*
ZDP	*Zeitschrift für Deutsche Philologie*

Introduction

1. Friedrich Beissner, *Der Erzähler Franz Kafka* (Stuttgart: W. Kohlhammer, 1952). The principle is elaborated by Martin Walser, *Beschreibung einer Form—Franz Kafka* (Munich: Carl Hanser, 1961), still the most important single monograph on Kafka's technique.

2. For example, Keith Leopold, "Breaks in Perspective in Franz Kafka's *Der Prozess*," *GQ*, 36 (1963), 31–38.

3. Jörgen Kobs, *Kafka: Untersuchungen zu Bewusstsein und Sprache seiner Gestalten* (Bad Homburg: Athenäum, 1970), pp. 19–25.

4. E.D. Hirsch Jr., *Validity in Interpretation* (New Haven: Yale University Press, 1967).

5. Evelyn Torton Beck, *Kafka and the Yiddish Theatre* (Madison: Wisconsin University Press, 1971).

6. The relevance of the theater to Kafka's work has been noticed in passing by many critics since Walter Benjamin's ground breaking essay. A recent example: "The place of the action reminds one of a stage where every prop has been placed in such a way that the spectator can concentrate his attention only on the figures of the work. Inanimate objects close around the man in a tight, monotonous circle in which there is no chink." Roman Karst, "Franz Kafka: Word-Space-Time," in *Mosaic*, 3 (1970), 8. My intention is to move beyond impressionism to systematic analysis of the problem.

7. *T*, 463; *D2*, 115.

8. J.M.S. Pasley, introduction to *Der Heizer. In der Strafkolonie. Der Bau* (Cambridge University Press, 1966), p. 13.

9. Walter Sokel, *Franz Kafka. Tragik und Ironie* (Munich: A. Langen-G. Müller, 1964). His views are concisely and even more impressively formulated in *Franz Kafka* (New York: Columbia University Press, 1966), the work quoted here.

10. Heinz Hillmann, *Franz Kafka—Dichtungstheorie und Dichtungsgestalt* (Bonn: H. Bouvier, 1965).

11. Heinz Politzer, *Parable and Paradox* (Ithaca: Cornell University Press, 1962).

12. Heinrich Wölfflin, *Principles of Art History* (New York: Dover, n.d.), p. 130.

13. The legitimacy of this method is supported in a volume edited by Norbert Miller, *Romananfänge: Versuch zu einer Poetik des Romans* (Berlin: Literarisches Colloquium, 1965). From Miller's introduction, pp. 8–9: "The author must, in his first sentence, neutralize the general idea and purpose of his book (or at least appear to do so), which could be realized in countless plots and fictional structures. . . . With the first sentence the fiction separates itself from reality in order to shape a world governed by its own laws."

14. Malcolm Pasley, "Zur äusseren Gestalt des 'Schloss'-Romans," in *Kafka-Symposion* (Berlin: Verlag Klaus Wagenbach, 1965), pp. 181–88.

Chapter 1   *"Description of a Struggle"*

1. This story is now available in a critical edition, *Beschreibung eines Kampfes: die zwei Fassungen*, eds. Ludwig Dietz and Max Brod (Frankfurt: S. Fischer, 1969). Since I shall be concerned with the differences between the two versions, and since the extant English version, by Tania and James Stern, is of Max Brod's earlier collated edition, the translations will frequently be my own.

2. Jörgen Kobs, who offers a detailed analysis of this passage (*Kafka: Untersuchungen*, pp. 7–19), would not agree that the changes are unimportant. But the focus of his study is on the epistemology of Kafka's sentence structure, whereas I am concerned rather with the fictional context.

3. "Wir sind nämlich so wie Baumstämme in Schnee. Sie liegen doch scheinbar nur glatt auf und man sollte sie mit kleinem Anstoss wegschieben können. Aber nein, das kann man nicht, denn sie sind fest mit dem Boden verbunden. Aber sieh, sogar das ist bloss scheinbar." *B*, 58; *BZF*, 122; the second version (*BZF*, 123) is less formal, more consciously "spoken."

4. Wayne Booth, *The Rhetoric of Fiction* (Chicago University Press, 1961), pp. 59–60.

5. *B*, 293–94.

6. Judith Ryan, "Die zwei Fassungen der 'Beschreibung eines Kampfes,'" *Jahrbuch der deutschen Schillergesellschaft*, 14 (1970), 556.

7. Beda Allemann, "Der Prozess," in *Der deutsche Roman*, vol. 2, ed. Benno von Wiese (Düsseldorf: Bagel, 1963), pp. 234–90.

8. *B*, 7–8.

9. The Sterns translate *daher* as "whereupon," missing the incongruous causality.

10. "Kaum waren wir ins Freie getreten, als ich offenbar in grosse Munterkeit gerieth." *B*, 10.

11. Dorrit Cohn, "K. enters *The Castle:* on the change of person in Kafka's manuscript," *Euphorion*, 62 (1968), 28–45.

12. "Wieder stand ich still, als hätte ich im Stillstehen mehr Kraft des Urteils." Compare final version, *S*, 16.

13. Compare Ingeborg Henel, "Die Deutbarkeit von Kafkas Werken," *ZPD*, 86 (1967), 259: "The reader must follow this to-ing and fro-ing, the repeated dissociation of facts and assertions, without stopping at any point, even at assertions seemingly corresponding to a tangible philosophy."

14. *H*, 11–12 (my translation).

15. "Nur um dagegen nicht hilflos zu erscheinen, hatte ich mir meine Lustigkeit abgequält." *BZF*, 14.

16. "Ich fand .... Ich erinnerte mich ... wurde ein wenig lustiger fast hoch-

müthig kann man sagen . . . bildete mir ein, ich gienge selbstständig spazieren."
BZF, 16.

17. Judith Ryan, "Die zwei Fassungen," 568.

18. *B*, 11–12; the standard text follows the second version in dividing the paragraph into two. Compare *BZF*, 16–19.

19. *BZF*, 20. This paragraph is much altered and, to my mind, weakened in the second version, the nervous discontinuities of struggle being replaced by an unlikely but leisurely dialogue.

20. "Er aber gieng lächelnd auf meine Redeweise ein: 'Ja, Sie haben Recht, eine solche Nacht will nicht im Bette verschlafen sein.' " *BZF*, 20.

21. "Wissen Sie, wie Sie sind, komisch sind Sie." "Ich folgte ihm, ohne es zu merken, denn mich beschäftigte sein Ausspruch." *BZF*, 20.

22. First version: "Ich sah meinen Bekannten mit liebevollen Augen an. In Gedanken schützte ich ihn gegen Gefahren, besonders gegen Nebenbuhler und eifersüchtige Männer. Sein Leben wurde mir theuerer als meines. Ich fand sein Gesicht schön und ich war stolz auf sein Glück bei den Frauenzimmern und ich nahm an den Küssen theil, die er an diesem Abend von den zwei Mädchen bekommen hatte. Oh, dieser Abend war lustig!" *BZF*, 20, 22. Second version: "Dass mir ihn nur die Mädchen nicht verderben! Mögen sie ihn küssen und drücken, das ist ja ihre Pflicht und sein Recht, aber entführen sollen sie mir ihn nicht. Wenn sie ihn küssen, küssen sie mich ja auch ein wenig, wenn man will . . . . Und wie wenn er jetzt fällt, wie, wenn er sich verkühlt, wie, wenn ein Eifersüchtiger aus der Postgasse heraus ihn überfällt? Was soll dann mit mir geschehn, soll ich dann aus der Welt herausgeworfen werden? Das möchte ich doch sehn, nein, mich wird er nicht mehr los werden." *BZF*, 21, 23; *B*, 13–14.

23. First version: "Ich sah nicht, dass er erstaunt war, als er sich mitleidig zu mir bückte und mich mit weicher Hand streichelte." *BZF*, 34. Second version: "Ich merkte nicht, dass er überrascht war, als er sich zu mir bückte—er senkte fast nur den Hals ganz wie eine Hyäne—und mich mit weicher Hand streichelte." *BZF*, 35; *B*, 20.

24. "So redete ich und suchte krampfhaft hinter den Worten Liebesgeschichten mit merkwürdigen Lagen zu erfinden." *BZF*, 24.

25. "This reappearance of myth in the ironic is particularly clear in Kafka and in Joyce." Northrop Frye, *Anatomy of Criticism* (Princeton University Press, 1957), p. 42.

26. *Briefe an Felice*, ed. Erich Heller and Jürgen Born (New York, Frankfurt: S. Fischer, 1967), p. 252.

27. "Endlich glitt ich auf den Fusspitzen zum Türgang, gab dem blinden Bettler, der dort sass, eine Münze und drückte mich neben ihn hinter den geöffneten Türflügel." *BZF*, 80–81; *B*, 37. Although the changes are insignificant, the language is of the second version, in which the fat man does not appear. The implications of this reduction in the number of speakers apparently visualized by Kafka are discussed by Judith Ryan; my feeling, evidently shared by Brod in the production of the collated version, is that the multiplicity of perspectives, however illusory, is essential to the story's whimsical texture.

28. *BZF*, 78–79; *B*, 36.

Chapter 2   Open Structure: "The Stoker"

1. Pasley, *Kafka-Symposion*, pp. 62–63.

2. *Briefe an Felice*, p. 332.

3. *T*, 535–36; *D2*, 188.

4. Jörgen Kobs, *Kafka*, p. 437.

5. *T*, 481; *D2*, 132.

6. Pasley, introduction to *Der Heizer*, p. 13.

7. Frank Kermode, *The Sense of an Ending* (New York: Oxford University Press, 1967), p. 54.

8. *A*, 11.

9. *A*, 13.

10. *A*, 14–15.

11. Jörg Thalmann, *Wege zu Kafka. Eine Interpretation von Kafkas Amerikaroman* (Frauenfeld: Huber, 1966), p. 19.

12. "Jetzt hing alles vom Benehmen des Heizers ab, denn was die Gerechtigkeit seiner Sache anlangte, an der zweifelte Karl nicht." *A*, 22–23.

13. Wolfgang Jahn, *Kafkas Roman 'Der Verschollene'* (Stuttgart: Metzler, 1965), pp. 86–87.

14. "Bei dieser Stelle starrte Karl mit aller Kraft den Kapitän an, zutunlich, als sei er sein Kollege, nur damit er sich durch die etwas ungeschickte Ausdrucksweise des Heizers nicht zu dessen Ungunsten beeinflussen lasse." *A*, 24.

15. "Aber der Heizer missverstand das, witterte wohl in Karl irgendwelche geheime Vorwürfe gegen sich." *A*, 27.

16. Clemens Heselhaus, "Kafkas Erzählformen," *DVLG*, 26 (1952).

17. *A*, 40.

18. My translations. Although "playful" is not a very satisfactory equivalent, Muir omits the resonance of "play" in both contexts.

19. Walser, *Beschreibung einer Form*, p. 96.

20. *T*, 168; *D1*, 157.

Chapter 3   "The Urban World": The Experience of the Theater

1. *T*, 45–52; *D1*, 47–54.

2. *D1*, 47–48.

3. "Das, was man ist, kann man nicht ausdrücken, denn dieses ist man eben; mitteilen kann man nur das, was man nicht ist, also die Lüge. Erst im Chor mag eine gewisse Wahrheit liegen." *H*, 343.

4. Eberhard Lämmert, *Bauformen des Erzählens*, 3rd ed. (Stuttgart: Metzler, 1968), p. 97.

5. *T*, 161; *D1*, 151.

6. *T*, 187; *D1*, 174.

7. *T*, 339; *D1*, 318.

8. *T*, 550; *D2*, 200.

9. "Aus Erdenschwere." *H*, 43.

10. *T*, 129; *D1*, 123.

11. Evelyn Torton Beck, in *Kafka and the Yiddish Theatre*, argues just this point; but although the detailed parallels she adduces are striking indeed, the same has long been known to be true of parallels between Kafka's personal life and the life of his heroes. Kafka enjoyed teasing readers about his sources. But the more we know about these sources, the less they seem to "explain" about the autonomous worlds of Kafka's fiction.

12. The importance of this passage has been underlined by R.G. Collins: "in speaking of drama, he talked about art as he himself was to pursue it." "Kafka's Special Methods of Thinking," *Mosaic*, 3 (1970), 52.

13. *T*, 219–20; *D1*, 203.

14. *T*, 124; *D1*, 118–19.

15. *T*, 124; *D1*, 119.

16. "Verstecke sind unzählige, Rettung nur eine, aber Möglichkeiten der Rettung wieder so viele wie Verstecke." *H*, 41 (my translation).

Chapter 4   *"The Judgment"*

1. Sokel, *Franz Kafka*, pp. 19–24.

2. Lawrence Ryan, " 'Zum letzten Mal Psychologie!' Zur psychologischen Deutbarkeit der Werke Franz Kafkas," *Psychologie in der Literaturwissenschaft* (Heidelberg: L. Stiehm, 1971), p. 165.

3. *T*, 296; *D1*, 278. Subsequent phrases of commentary by Kafka quoted in the text are also taken from this diary entry for 11 February 1913. Sometimes, where Kresh's version seems to miss the immediacy of Kafka's self-analysis, I have substituted my own efforts.

4. The Muir translation, as noted earlier, misses this resonance, offering instead "dreamy."

5. Sokel, *Franz Kafka*, p. 24.

6. My translation. Muir renders "richtete sich ein" as "resigned himself," thereby weighting the neutral verb in the direction of Georg's own bias. It is my contention that Kafka is deliberately conveying information at this point for which neutral language is appropriate.

7. The term is Walter Benjamin's; his remarkable essay on Kafka is printed in

Illuminations, ed. Hannah Arendt (New York: Schocken Books, 1968), pp. 111–40. The phrase "swamp world," discussion of which begins on p. 130, refers to what he sees as the "prehistoric" quality of the novels, the anonymous instinctuality of so many of the characters; but the interdependence of the hero and his world suggests that the ruthless rationality engendered by modern civilization is itself a renewed manifestation of the swamp world, a breaking-down of the precarious human balance.

8. "Von dem Todesfall von Georgs Mutter . . . hatte der Freund wohl noch erfahren und sein Beileid in einem Brief mit einer Trockenheit ausgedrückt, die ihren Grund nur darin haben konnte, dass die Trauer über ein solches Ereignis in der Fremde ganz unvorstellbar wird." *E*, 55.

9. Again, Muir's rendering, "of course," dispels some essential shadows. The word may be untranslatable—clearly the friend *did* hear of the event but, equally clearly, Georg was not his source. "Surely" might be preferable.

10. "Er wollte nichts anderes als die Vorstellung ungestört lassen, die sich der Freund von der Heimatstadt in der langen Zwischenzeit wohl gemacht und mit welcher er sich abgefunden hatte." *E*, 56.

11. "So geschah es Georg, dass er dem Freund die Verlobung eines gleichgültigen Menschen mit einem ebenso gleichgültigen Mädchen dreimal in ziemlich weit auseinanderliegenden Briefen anzeigte." *E*, 56.

12. "Wenn du solche Freunde hast, Georg, hättest du dich überhaupt nicht verloben sollen." *E*, 57. Again I have altered Muir's phrasing, which reads, "Since your friends are like that . . ."; throughout this story he seems concerned to establish a logical, coherent "tone," whereas the pregnant neutrality of the language, the abrupt shifts in focus, have a vital part in suggesting the abyss that is about to open up.

13. Again the phrase is from Kafka's own commentary. *T*, 296–97; *D1*, 279.

14. " 'Aber schau mich an!' rief der Vater, und Georg lief, fast zerstreut, zum Bett, um alles zu fassen, stockte aber in der Mitte des Weges." *E*, 64.

Chapter 5   *"The Metamorphosis"*

1. Sokel's term.

2. Lawrence Ryan, " 'Zum letzten Mal Psychologie!'," pp. 165–66.

3. *E*, 72.

4. "Gregor aber dachte gar nicht daran aufzumachen, sondern lobte die vom Reisen her übernommene Vorsicht, auch zu Hause alle Türen während der Nacht zu versperren." *E*, 75. Again I have altered the first phrase of the Muir translation, which simply misses the force of "dachte gar nicht daran."

5. "Zunächst wollte er ruhig und ungestört aufstehen, sich anziehen und vor allem frühstücken, und dann erst das Weitere überlegen, denn, das merkte er wohl, im Bett würde er mit dem Nachdenken zu keinem vernünftigen Ende kommen." *E*, 75.

6. "Aber als er wieder nach gleicher Mühe aufseufzend so dalag wie früher,

und wieder seine Beinchen womöglich noch ärger gegeneinander kämpfen sah und keine Möglichkeit fand, in diese Willkür Ruhe und Ordnung zu bringen, sagte er sich wieder, dass er unmöglich im Bett bleiben könne und dass es das Vernünftigste sei, alles zu opfern, wenn auch nur die kleinste Hoffnung bestünde, sich dadurch vom Bett zu befreien. Gleichzeitig aber vergass er nicht, sich zwischendurch daran zu erinnern, dass viel besser als verzweifelte Entschlüsse ruhige und ruhigste Überlegung sei." *E*, 77. My point about the frequency of "Ruhe" and "ruhig" is perhaps inevitably lost in the translation.

7. "Und ein Weilchen lang lag er ruhig mit schwachem Atem, als erwarte er vielleicht von der völligen Stille die Wiederkehr der wirklichen und selbstverständlichen Verhältnisse." *E*, 77.

8. *E*, 81.

9. "Gregor schien es, dass es viel vernünftiger wäre, ihn jetzt in Ruhe zu lassen, statt ihn mit Weinen und Zureden zu stören." *E*, 82.

10. *E*, 90–91.

11. Benno von Wiese, "Franz Kafka, 'Die Verwandlung'," in *Die deutsche Novelle von Goethe bis Kafka*, vol. 2 (Düsseldorf: Bagel, 1962), p. 334.

12. Georg Lukacs, *The Meaning of Contemporary Realism*, (London: Merlin Press, 1962), p. 25.

13. "Im gegenteiligen Fall, der sich allmählich immer häufiger wiederholte." *E*, 100.

14. *E*, 67.

15. *E*, 96.

16. "Wie aber, wenn jetzt alle Ruhe, aller Wohlstand, alle Zufriedenheit ein Ende mit Schrecken nehmen sollte?" *E*, 95.

17. Politzer stresses this parallelism, but regards the story's final symmetry as an aesthetic error: "The title of the story might apply to Grete with greater justification than to Gregor, for it is her metamorphosis which is developed in the course of the narrative, whereas we have to accept Gregor's as an accomplished fact. More and more she plays herself into the foreground: the end will show her transformation completed, very much to the detriment of the story." *Parable and Paradox*, p. 74. Hartmut Binder's investigation of the problem of perspective, however, leads to the conclusion that Kafka has broadened Gregor's viewpoint to such an extent that the caesura of his death is more apparent than real: "The epilogue is by no means inorganic, but merely the continuation of the second narrative strand which was always present and which had already, although from Gregor's perspective, been presented with the same neutrality: a fact that reveals itself, for example, in the reader's experience that the change of perspective at the conclusion of the story involves no change in the modalities of perception." *Motiv und Gestaltung bei Franz Kafka* (Bonn: H. Bouvier, 1966), p. 295.

18. Stanley Corngold stresses the charwoman's role in this dialectic; the very strangeness of her hardened "normality" propels the reader into reevaluating the effects of the metamorphosis: "The cleaning woman does not know that a

metamorphosis has occurred, that in this insect shape there is a human consciousness, one superior at times to the ordinary consciousness of Gregor Samsa." "Kafka's *Die Verwandlung*: Metamorphosis of the Metaphor," in *Mosaic*, 3 (1970), 98.

19. *E*, 98.

20. "Die Schwester suchte freilich die Peinlichkeit des Ganzen möglichst zu verwischen, und je längere Zeit verging, desto besser gelang es ihr natürlich auch, aber auch Gregor durchschaute mit der Zeit alles viel genauer. Schon ihr Eintritt war für ihn schrecklich." *E*, 105.

21. *E*, 106–7.

22. *E*, 111.

23. *E*, 112.

24. "Das Licht auf dem zurückweichenden Fratzengesicht ist wahr, sonst nichts." *H*, 46.

25. "Er wunderte sich kaum darüber, dass er in letzter Zeit so wenig Rucksicht auf die andern nahm; früher war diese Rücksichtnahme sein Stolz gewesen." *E*, 129.

26. Heselhaus, "Kafkas Erzählformen," p. 357.

27. Politzer's interpretation of this scene is diametrically opposed to mine: "Even in this moment of dedicated listening he cannot accept music for what it is; he has to translate it into images of concrete possession which is all that he understands.... We have arrived at the vertex of the story which, thanks to Kafka's masterful counterpoint, is also the low point in the insect's development. We feel the icy breath of an existence fatally gone astray." *Parable and Paradox*, p. 77. But if this is the low point, where are the high points? Despite Politzer's lip service to the story's structural movement, basically his view of Gregor is statically behavioristic; he sees only one aspect of a situation where Kafka's systematic deployment of antithesis has invariably built in a counter-element. Above all, he does not distinguish between the banal substance of Gregor's life and the "transformation" of that life through the hero's reenactment of it: "The metamorphosis has failed to change him. He dies, as he lived, a thing" (p. 79). And yet Gregor's death is the moment at which the reader feels most strongly the ambivalence of the story's physical outcome. By positing some unrealistic, quasimystical notion of "inward change," Politzer fails to notice the substantive change that is actually taking place in Gregor, through his unyielding fidelity to his own past.

28. *E*, 132.

29. Jürg Schubiger, *"Die Verwandlung"—eine Interpretation* (Zurich: Atlantis, 1969), p. 52.

30. Günther Anders, *Kafka Pro und contra* (Munich: C.H. Beck, 1951), p. 20.

31. Wilhelm Emrich, *Franz Kafka* (Bonn: Athenäum, 1958), p. 127.

32. Wilhelm Emrich, *Franz Kafka*, p. 123.

Chapter 6   Closed Structure: The Trial

1. Hillmann, *Franz Kafka—Dichtungstheorie*, p. 77.

2. Fritz Martini, *Das Wagnis der Sprache* (Stuttgart: Klett, 1954), pp. 293–94.

3. Walser, *Beschreibung einer Form*, pp. 117–18, 120–21. Ingeborg Henel draws extreme conclusions from this thesis: "Even the people in this world are not derived from the empirical world, they are, as Walser has shown, neither psychologically true, nor anthropologically human, nor biologically natural. Their character is defined exclusively by their function." ("Die Deutbarkeit von Kafkas Werken," *ZDP*, 86 [1967], 254.) This statement, while truer of *The Trial* than of Kafka's subsequent works, begs the common-sense question: why does the reader accept the human logic of the characters' responses, why does *The Trial* stubbornly resist the arbitrary associations of the dream world? Granted that this novel carries to an extreme the stylization of the empirical world common to all fiction, it also observes the minimum mimetic conventions without which the reader will not agree to enter into the "conversation" (Lämmert) of literary involvement. Walser's insights into Kafka's fictional method should not be transformed into yet another philosophical schema, however anti-idealistic.

4. Gesine Frey, *Der Raum und die Figuren in Franz Kafkas Roman "Der Prozess"* (Marburg: Elwert, 1965), p. 181.

5. Allemann, "Der Prozess," pp. 238–39.

6. Sokel, *Franz Kafka*, p. 29.

7. *T*, 414–15; *D2*, 71–72.

8. "Er neigte stets dazu, alles möglichst leicht zu nehmen, das Schlimmste erst beim Eintritt des Schlimmsten zu glauben, keine Vorsorge für die Zukunft zu treffen, selbst wenn alles drohte." *P*, 12.

9. "... trotzdem war er diesmal, förmlich schon seit dem ersten Anblick des Wächters Franz, entschlossen, nicht den geringsten Vorteil, den er vielleicht gegenüber diesen Leuten besass, aus der Hand zu geben." *P*, 13.

10. My translation. The Muirs introduce overtones not present in the original in their rendering of the main clause, "he would insist on playing it to the end."

11. "... versuchte, zunächst stillschweigend, durch Aufmerksamkeit und Überlegung festzustellen, wer der Mann eigentlich war." *P*, 9.

12. "Ich will doch sehen, was für Leute im Nebenzimmer sind und wie Frau Grubach diese Störung mir gegenüber verantworten wird." *P*, 9.

13. The Muirs add the word "ridiculous"—"in such a ridiculous fashion"—thereby inflecting K.'s words in a direction not specified in the text.

14. " '[Das Gesetz] besteht wohl auch nur in Ihren Köpfen,' sagte K., er wollte sich irgendwie in die Gedanken der Wächter einschleichen." *P*, 15.

15. "K. liess sich, ohne es zu wollen, in ein Zwiegespräch der Blicke mit Franz ein, schlug dann aber doch auf seine Papiere." *P*, 14.

16. Benjamin, in *Illuminations*, ed. Arendt, pp. 124, 131.

17. " 'Es hilft nichts,' sagten die Wächter, die immer, wenn K. schrie, ganz ruhig, ja fast traurig wurden und ihn dadurch verwirrten oder gewissermassen zur Besinnung brachten." *P*, 18.

18. "K. warf daraufhin den Rock zu Boden und sagte—er wusste selbst nicht, in welchem Sinne er es sagte—: 'Es ist doch noch nicht die Hauptverhandlung.' " *P*, 18. The Muirs render "Hauptverhandlung" as "capital charge," flattening out the ambivalence of K.'s remark, which implies a certain relish at the prospect of participating in a "comedy."

19. "Er beobachtete sie, ob sie sich vielleicht daran doch erinnern würden, aber das fiel ihnen natürlich gar nicht ein." *P*, 19.

20. The Muirs render this as "roving glance," which sounds too purposeful.

21. "Gewiss, ich bin überrascht, aber ich bin keineswegs sehr überrascht." *P*, 20.

22. "... wandte sich hierbei an alle und hätte gern sogar die drei bei den Photographien sich zugewendet." *P*, 21.

23. "Der Aufseher stimmte ihm möglicherweise zu, wie K. mit einem Seitenblick zu erkennen glaubte. Aber es war ebensogut möglich, dass er gar nicht zugehört hatte." *P*, 23.

24. Karl J. Kuepper points to the obsessiveness of this motif: "the gesture of shaking hands occurs so frequently in *The Trial* that it must be seen in a larger context." "Gesture and Posture as Elemental Symbolism in Kafka's *The Trial*," in *Mosaic*, 3 (1970), 146.

25. "Er spielte mit ihnen. Er hatte die Absicht, falls sie weggehen sollten, bis zum Haustor nachzulaufen und ihnen seine Verhaftung anzubieten." *P*, 24.

26. "... untergeordnete Beamte aus der Bank waren es allerdings. Wie hatte K. das übersehen können? ... Viel Geistesgegenwart bewies das nicht, und K. nahm sich vor, sich in dieser Hinsicht genauer zu beobachten." *P*, 25, 27. Again I have made a change in the Muir translation to underline the mechanism of K.'s thoughts as conveyed by Kafka's original text. For "sich genauer beobachten," the Muirs offer the colorless "be more careful."

27. *P*, 27.

28. *P*, 305.

29. "Hätte ich vernünftig gehandelt, so wäre nichts weiter geschehen, es wäre alles, was werden wollte, erstickt worden." *P*, 31.

30. Frey, *Der Raum und die Figuren*, p. 25.

31. *P*, 36.

32. "Die Untersuchungskommission kann doch eingesehen haben, dass ich unschuldig bin oder doch nicht so schuldig, wie angenommen wurde." *P*, 37. I have altered the Muir translation which, at this point, is simply inaccurate.

33. Frey, *Der Raum und die Figuren*, p. 27.

34. In the Cathedral chapter the priest *does* shout his name; this kind of prefiguration is to be found everywhere in *The Trial*, adding both variety and density to the circular motion of the individual chapters. Indeed, if one may discount the controversy about the order of the chapters, a kind of pyramidal or mirror-

structure can be discerned in the sequence of ten as we have them. The detailing of the first chapter is repeatedly echoed in chapters nine and ten together; in chapters two and eight Josef K. adopts an aggressive attitude, in chapters three and seven he attempts to modulate his role into a defensive, "observing" posture. In chapters four and six he seeks allies, which leaves the fifth chapter ("The Whipper") as the parabolic center, in which K. is forced into unmediated contact with the implications of his situation; this chapter mirrors itself in the inexplicable repetition of the whipping scene. All the variants of his role developed by K. are of course systematically nullified by the Court.

35. *P*, 41.

36. "Das Gericht will nichts von dir. Es nimmt dich auf, wenn du kommst, und es entlässt dich, wenn du gehst." *P*, 265.

37. Anders puts it strikingly: "Objects are frozen truths." *Kafka Pro und contra*, p. 55.

Chapter 7   Closed Structure: "In the Penal Colony"

1. Hellmuth Kaiser, "Franz Kafkas Inferno, eine psychologische Deutung seiner Strafphantasie," *Imago*, 17 (1931), 37.

2. Ulrich Fülleborn, "Zum Verhältnis von Perspektivismus und Parabolik in der Dichtung Kafkas," in *Wissenschaft als Dialog: Festschrift für Wolfdietrich Rasch* (Stuttgart: Metzler, 1969), p. 301.

3. Wilhelm Emrich, *Protest und Verheissung: Studien zur klassischen und modernen Dichtung* (Frankfurt: Athenäum, 1960), p. 236.

4. "Der Reisende schien nur aus Höflichkeit der Einladung des Kommandanten gefolgt zu sein . . . ging hinter dem Verurteilten fast sichtbar unbeteiligt auf und ab." *E*, 199.

5. *E*, 199.

6. "Der Reisende war schon ein wenig für den Apparat gewonnen; die Hand zum Schutz gegen die Sonne über den Augen, sah er an dem Apparat in die Höhe." *E*, 203.

7. ". . . da er die Hand nicht über die Augen legen konnte, blinzelte er mit freien Augen zur Höhe." *E*, 204.

8. " 'Nun liegt also der Mann,' sagte der Reisende, lehnte sich im Sessel zurück und kreuzte die Beine." *E*, 204.

9. My use of the word "totalitarian" seeks to relate its obvious and appropriate modern connotations to a permanently latent world-view at the opposite pole from liberal individualism; the Inquisition, for example, as interpreted for Kafka by Dostoevsky, claimed "total" authority over every detail of an individual's life.

10. *E*, 205.

11. "Der Reisende hatte Verschiedenes fragen wollen, fragte aber im Anblick des Mannes nur: 'Kennt er sein Urteil?' . . . Der Reisende wollte schon verstummen, da fühlte er, wie der Verurteilte seinen Blick auf ihn richtete; er schien zu fragen, ob er den geschilderten Vorgang billigen könne." *E*, 205–6. Although I

haven't altered the Muir translation, it is somewhat inadequate: the emotive word "troubling," in particular, suggests a "concern" in the explorer not indicated by Kafka's neutral terminology.

12. " 'Er muss doch Gelegenheit gehabt haben, sich zu verteidigen,' sagte der Reisende und stand vom Sessel auf." *E*, 206.

13. *E*, 208.

14. *E*, 209–10.

15. "... er streckte, während der Soldat mit seiner rechten Hand beschäftigt war, die linke aus, ohne zu wissen wohin; es war aber die Richtung, wo der Reisende stand." *E*, 213.

16. *E*, 215.

17. *E*, 216.

18. *E*, 219.

19. *E*, 221.

20. *E*, 222.

21. "Die Antwort, die er zu geben hatte, war für den Reisenden von allem Anfang an zweifellos; er hatte in seinem Leben zu viel erfahren, als dass er hier hätte schwanken können; er war im Grunde ehrlich und hatte keine Furcht. Trotzdem zögerte er jetzt im Anblick des Soldaten und des Verurteilten einen Atemzug lang. Schliesslich aber sagte er, wie er musste: 'Nein ... Sie haben es mir noch klarer gemacht, ohne aber etwa meinen Entschluss erst befestigt zu haben.' " *E*, 225–26.

22. *E*, 230.

23. *E*, 233–34.

24. *E*, 234.

25. Kaiser, "Franz Kafkas Inferno," p. 62.

Chapter 8	*The Functional and the Arbitrary: "The Village Schoolteacher" and "The Great Wall of China"*

1. For example, Matthew Hodgart, "K." *New York Review of Books 12* (10 April 1969), 3–4.

2. This book might have been mentioned much earlier, and with a more literal relevance, in connection with the "Diversions" in "Description of a Struggle." There the narrator moves nature around at whim—and feels threatened by the result. Again a continuity becomes apparent between Kafka's early theme of human perception and the techniques he later employs simultaneously to build up and destroy his narrative voices.

3. In the standard translation this story is entitled "The Giant Mole," from Kafka's alternative title, "Der Riesenmaulwurf." I have elected to use the title employed by Kafka himself in discussing the work in his diary entry for December 1914 (*T*, 449–53). Both stories are contained in *B*, 57–83, 220–39.

4. "Zur Vermeidung eines Wortirrtums: Was tätig zerstört werden soll, muss vorher ganz fest gehalten worden sein; was zerbröckelt, zerbröckelt, kann aber nicht zerstört werden." *H*, 50 (my translation).

5. Compare Beck, *Kafka and the Yiddish Theatre*, chapter on "The Judgment."

6. "Er zog den Brief ein wenig aus der Tasche und liess ihn wieder zurückfallen." *E*, 59. "Vorläufig hielt ich dieses Rundschreiben noch mit den Händen verdeckt." *B*, 234.

7. "Das Wort 'sein' bedeutet im Deutschen beides: Dasein und Ihmgehören." *H*, 44 (my translation).

8. Kobs, *Kafka: Untersuchungen*, p. 19.

Chapter 9   Reopened Structure: The Castle

1. Hillmann, *Franz Kafka—Dichtungstheorie*, p. 77.

2. Walser, *Beschreibung einer Form*, pp. 105–6.

3. Sokel, *Franz Kafka*, pp. 42–43.

4. Klaus-Peter Philippi, *Reflexion und Wirklichkeit. Untersuchungen zu Kafkas Roman "Das Schloss"* (Tübingen: Niemeyer, 1966), p. 35.

5. Bluma Goldstein, "Key Motifs in Franz Kafka's 'Der Prozess' and 'Das Schloss' " (Ph.D. dissertation, Radcliffe, 1962), pp. 77–78.

6. Walser, *Beschreibung einer Form*, p. 100.

7. My translation; the Muir version is rather pale.

8. Hillmann, *Franz Kafka—Dichtungstheorie*, p. 191.

9. "Im einzelnen überraschte es K., im ganzen hatte er es freilich erwartet." *S*, 8.

10. "K. blieb wie bisher, drehte sich nicht einmal um, schien gar nicht neugierig, sah vor sich hin." *S*, 9.

11. *S*, 9.

12. My translation; the Muirs miss the tactical nuance of "alles Nötige."

13. *S*, 14.

14. *S*, 12.

15. The Muir translation, "I like to be my own master," sacrifices the resonances of the word *frei* in the interest of a conversational tone.

16. *S*, 157.

17. "Wieder stand K. still, als hätte er im Stillestehen mehr Kraft des Urteils." *S*, 16.

18. *H*, 352 (my translation).

19. ". . . endlich riss er sich los von dieser festhaltenden Strasse, ein schmales Gässchen nahm ihn auf." *S*, 18.

20. *S*, 19.

21. "Um sie herum spielten ein paar Kinder ... Die Frau beim Waschtrog, blond, in jugendlicher Fülle, sang leise bei der Arbeit." *S*, 20.

22. "... ich komme mir förmlich wie ungeboren vor, selbst ein Dunkles, jage ich im Dunkeln." *Br*, 178 (my translation).

23. *T*, 561; *D2*, 210.

24. *T*, 566; *D2*, 215.

*Chapter 10   Historical Structure:
         "Josefine the Singer, or the Mouse Folk"*

1. For consistency I employ the German spelling of Josefine's name.

2. "Josefine behauptet sich, dieses Nichts an Stimme, dieses Nichts an Leistung behauptet sich und schafft sich den Weg zu uns." *E*, 278.

3. "Es gibt ein Ziel, aber keinen Weg; was wir Weg nennen, ist Zögern." *H*, 42.

4. Fülleborn, "Zum Verhältnis von Perspektivismus," p. 291.

5. *E*, 271–72.

6. *E*, 269.

7. *E*, 277.

8. My translation; the Muir version irons out the paradox.

9. Emrich, *Franz Kafka*, p. 172.

10. *E*, 282.

11. *E*, 282.

12. *E*, 283–84.

13. *E*, 286.

14. *E*, 271.

15. *E*, 284.

16. *E*, 287.

17. *E*, 290.

Sources Consulted

This list includes only what, in the author's opinion, constitutes the basic Kafka "reading list," together with certain items of special significance for the foregoing study. For a comprehensive bibliography see Harry Järv, *Die Kafka-Literatur, Eine Bibliographie* (Malmö, Lund, 1961). This is usefully supplemented by a bibliography of Kafka criticism in English, 1960–1970, in *Modern Fiction Studies 17* (Spring 1971). *Franz Kafka Today*, edited by Flores and Swander (see below), contains a substantial bibliography; among general essays available in English, the most stimulating are those by Walter Benjamin and Walter Sokel.

Primary Sources

The following are the volumes of the standard German edition of Kafka's *Gesammelte Werke* edited by Max Brod, unless others are indicated. All are published by S. Fischer Verlag, Frankfurt, under license from Schocken Books, New York.

Amerika (1953).

Beschreibung eines Kampfes: Die zwei Fassungen, ed. Ludwig Dietz and Max Brod (1969).

Beschreibung eines Kampfes. Novellen, Skizzen, Aphorismen aus dem Nachlass (1954).

Briefe 1902–1924 (1958).

Briefe an Felice, ed. Erich Heller and Jürgen Born (1967).

Briefe an Milena, ed. Willy Haas (1952).

Erzählungen (1952).

Hochzeitsvorbereitungen auf dem Lande und andere Prosa aus dem Nachlass (1954).

Der Prozess (1950).

Das Schloss (1951).

Tagebücher (1951).

The American editions used are:

America. Translated by Edwin Muir. New York: New Directions, 1946.

The Castle. Translated by Willa and Edwin Muir with additional materials translated by Eithne Wilkins and Ernst Kaiser. New York: Alfred A. Knopf, 1954.

Dearest Father, stories and other writings. Translated by Ernst Kaiser and Eithne Wilkins. New York: Schocken Books, 1954.

Description of a Struggle. Translated by Tania and James Stern. New York: Schocken Books, 1958.

Diaries, 1910–1913. Translated by Joseph Kresh. New York: Schocken Books, 1948.

Diaries, 1914–1923. Translated by Martin Greenberg in cooperation with Hannah Arendt. New York: Schocken Books, 1949.

The Great Wall of China. Translated by Willa and Edwin Muir. New York: Schocken Books, 1946. Includes: "The Great Wall of China" and "The Village Schoolteacher."

The Penal Colony. Translated by Willa and Edwin Muir. New York: Schocken Books, 1948.

The Trial. Translated by Willa and Edwin Muir with additional materials translated by E.M. Butler. New York: Alfred A. Knopf, 1957.

Secondary Sources

Allemann, Beda. "Kafka: Der Prozess," in *Der deutsche Roman*, vol. 2. Edited by Benno von Wiese. Düsseldorf: Bagel, 1963, pp. 234–90.

Anders, Günther. *Kafka Pro und contra*. Munich: C.H. Beck, 1951.

Beck, Evelyn Torton. *Kafka and the Yiddish Theatre*. Madison: Wisconsin University Press, 1971.

Beissner, Friedrich. *Der Erzähler Franz Kafka*. Stuttgart: W. Kohlhammer, 1952.

———. *Kafka der Dichter*. Stuttgart: W. Kohlhammer, 1958.

———. *Der Schacht von Babel*. Stuttgart: W. Kohlhammer, 1963.

Benjamin, Walter. "Franz Kafka: eine Würdigung," in *Jüdische Rundschau 102* (1934). Translated by Harry Zohn in *Illuminations*. Edited by Hannah Arendt. New York: Schocken Books, 1968, pp. 111–140.

Binder, Hartmut. *Motiv und Gestaltung bei Franz Kafka*. Bonn: H. Bouvier, 1966.

Booth, Wayne C. *The Rhetoric of Fiction*. Chicago University Press, 1961.

Cohn, Dorrit. "K. Enters *The Castle*: on the Change of Person in Kafka's Manuscript," *Euphorion*, 62 (1968), 28–45.

Collins, R. G. "Kafka's Special Methods of Thinking," *Mosaic*, 3 (1970), 43–57.

Corngold, Stanley. "Kafka's *Die Verwandlung*: Metamorphosis of the Metaphor," *Mosaic*, 3 (1970), 91–106.

Emrich, Wilhelm. *Franz Kafka*. Bonn: Athenäum, 1958.

———. *Franz Kafka*. Translated by S.Z. Büehne. New York: Ungar, 1968.

———. "Franz Kafkas Bruch mit der Tradition und sein neues Gesetz;" "Die Bilderwelt Franz Kafkas," in *Protest und Verheissung: Studien zur klassischen und modernen Dichtung*. Frankfurt: Athenäum, 1960, pp. 233–63.

———. "Kritik und Kafka." *NDH*, 110 (1966), 124–38. A review of studies by Heinz Politzer and Walter H. Sokel.

Flores, Angel, ed. *The Kafka Problem*. New York: New Directions, 1946.

Flores, Angel, and Swander, Homer, eds. *Franz Kafka Today*. Madison: Wisconsin University Press, 1958.

Frey, Gesine. *Der Raum und die Figuren in Franz Kafkas Roman "Der Prozess."* Marburg: Elwert, 1965.

Frye, Northrop. *Anatomy of Criticism*. Princeton University Press, 1957.

Fülleborn, Ulrich. "Zum Verhältnis von Perspektivismus und Parabolik in der Dichtung Kafkas," in *Wissenschaft als Dialog: Festschrift für Wolfdietrich Rasch*. Stuttgart: Metzler, 1969, pp. 289–312.

Goldstein, Bluma. "Key Motifs in Franz Kafka's 'Der Prozess' and 'Das Schloss'." Ph.D. dissertation, Radcliffe, 1962.

Gray, Ronald. *Kafka's Castle*. Cambridge University Press, 1956.

———, ed. *Kafka. A Collection of Critical Essays*. Englewood Cliffs, N.J.; Prentice Hall, 1962. Includes essays by Friedrich Beissner, Albert Camus, Edmund Wilson, Eliseo Vivas, Erich Heller, Austin Warren, et al.

Hasselblatt, Dieter. *Zauber und Logik. Zur Struktur des Dichterischen bei Kafka*. Cologne: Verlag Wissenschaft und Politik, 1964.

Henel, Heinrich. "Kafkas 'Der Bau,' or How to Escape from a Maze," *The Discontinuous Tradition: Studies in German in honour of E.L. Stahl*. Edited by P.F. Ganz. Oxford University Press, 1971, pp. 224–46.

Henel, Ingeborg. "Die Türhüterlegende und ihre Bedeutung für Kafkas *Prozess*," *DVLG*, 37 (1963), 50–70.

———. "Ein Hungerkünstler," *DVLG*, 38 (1964), 230–47.

———. "Die Deutbarkeit von Kafkas Werken," *ZDP*, 86 (1967), 250–66.

Heselhaus, Clemens. "Kafkas Erzählformen," *DVLG*, 26 (1952), 353–76.

Hillmann, Heinz. *Franz Kafka—Dichtungstheorie und Dichtungsgestalt*. Bonn: H. Bouvier, 1965.

Hirsch, E.D. Jr. *Validity in Interpretation*. New Haven: Yale University Press, 1967.

Ide, Heinz. "Franz Kafka, Der Prozess, Interpretation des ersten Kapitels," *Jahrbuch der Wittheit zu Bremen*, 6 (1962), 19–57.

Jahn, Wolfgang. *Kafkas Roman "Der Verschollene."* Stuttgart: Metzler, 1965.

Janouch, Gustav. *Gespräche mit Kafka,* rev. ed. Frankfurt: S. Fischer, 1968.

Kaiser, Hellmuth. "Franz Kafkas Inferno, eine psychologische Deutung seiner Strafphantasie," *Imago,* 17 (1931), 41–103.

Karst, Roman. "Franz Kafka: Word-Space-Time," *Mosaic,* 3 (1970), 1–13.

Kermode, Frank. *The Sense of an Ending.* New York: Oxford University Press, 1967.

Kobs, Jörgen. *Kafka: Untersuchungen zu Bewusstsein und Sprache seiner Gestalten.* Bad Homburg: Athenäum, 1970.

Kudszus, Winfried. "Erzählhaltung und Zeitverschiebung in Kafkas *Prozess* und *Schloss,*" *DVLG,* 38 (1964), 192–207.

———. "Erzählperspektive und Erzählgeschehen in Kafkas *Prozess,*" *DVLG,* 44 (1970), 306–17.

Kuepper, Karl J. "Gesture and Posture as Elemental Symbolism in Kafka's *The Trial,*" *Mosaic,* 3 (1970), 143–52.

Lämmert, Eberhard. *Bauformen des Erzählens.* Stuttgart: Metzler, 1955.

Leopold, Keith. "Breaks in Perspective in Franz Kafka's *Der Prozess,*" *GQ,* 36 (1963), 31–38.

Lukacs, Georg. *The Meaning of Contemporary Realism.* London: Merlin Press, 1962.

Martini, Fritz. "Ein Manuskript Franz Kafkas—Der Dorfschullehrer," *Jahrbuch der Deutschen Schillergesellschaft,* 2 (1958), 266–300.

———. "Franz Kafka, *Das Schloss,*" in *Das Wagnis der Sprache.* Stuttgart: Klett, 1954, pp. 287–335.

Miller, Norbert, ed. *Romananfänge: Versuch zu einer Poetik des Romans.* Berlin: Literarisches Colloquium, 1965.

Pasley, Malcolm, ed., with Jürgen Born, Ludwig Dietz, Paul Raabe, Klaus Wagenbach. *Kafka-Symposion.* Berlin: Verlag Klaus Wagenbach, 1965.

———. Introduction to *Der Heizer. In der Strafkolonie. Der Bau.* Cambridge University Press, 1966.

Philippi, Klaus-Peter. *Reflexion und Wirklichkeit, Untersuchungen zu Kafkas Roman "Das Schloss."* Tübingen: Niemeyer, 1966.

Politzer, Heinz. *Parable and Paradox.* Ithaca: Cornell University Press, 1962.

Ramm, Klaus. *Reduktion als Erzählprinzip bei Kafka.* Frankfurt: Athenäum, 1971.

Ryan, Judith. "Die zwei Fassungen der 'Beschreibung eines Kampfes'," *Jahrbuch der deutschen Schillergesellschaft,* 14 (1970), 546–72.

Ryan, Lawrence. " 'Zum letzten Mal Psychologie!' Zur psychologischen Deutbarkeit der Werke Franz Kafkas," *Psychologie in der Literaturwissenschaft.* Edited by Wolfgang Paulsen. Heidelberg: L. Stiehm, 1971, pp. 157–73.

Schillemeit, Jost. "Welt im Werk Franz Kafkas," *DVLG,* 38 (1964), 168–91.

———. "Zum Wirklichkeitsproblem der Kafka-Interpretation," *DVLG*, 40 (1966), 577–96.

Schubiger, Jürg. *"Die Verwandlung"—eine Interpretation*. Zurich: Atlantis, 1969.

Sokel, Walter H. *Franz Kafka. Tragik und Ironie*. Munich: A. Langen-G. Müller, 1964.

———. *Franz Kafka*. Columbia Essays on Modern Writers, no. 19. New York, 1966.

———. "Das Verhältnis der Erzählperspektive zu Erzählgeschehen und Sinngehalt in 'Vor dem Gesetz' 'Schakale und Araber' und 'Der Prozess'," *ZDP*, 86 (1967), 267–300.

Tauber, Herbert. *Franz Kafka; An Interpretation of His Works*. Translated by G. Humphreys Roberts and Roger Senhouse. New Haven: Yale University Press, 1948.

Thalmann, Jörg. *Wege zu Kafka. Eine Interpretation von Kafkas Amerika-Roman*. Frauenfeld: Huber, 1966.

Wagenbach, Klaus. *Franz Kafka. Eine Biographie seiner Jugend, 1883–1912*. Berne: Francke, 1958.

———. *Kafka in Selbstzeugnissen und Bilddokumenten*. Hamburg: Rowohlt, 1964.

Walser, Martin. *Beschreibung einer Form-Franz Kafka*. Munich: Carl Hanser, 1961.

Wiese, Benno von. "Franz Kafka, 'Die Verwandlung'," *Die deutsche Novelle von Goetherbis Kafka*, vol. 2. Düsseldorf: Bagel, 1962, pp. 319–45.

Wölfflin, Heinrich. *Principles of Art History*. New York: Dover, n.d.

Index of Kafka's Works and Characters

Index of Names